Critical Acclaim for **Prepare Your Own Will**

"**An excellent reference** for demystifying the will-making process, even for those who decide to hire a lawyer to handle the process. Preparing a will does not have to be done with the help of a lawyer. Sitarz offers this step-by-step guide to self-planning and preparation of a legal will. Besides **clear text**, Sitarz includes sample documents, a glossary of legal terms, and **pertinent checklists**. In addition, a state-by-state appendix of different (state) laws is **particularly useful**."

American Library Association Booklist

"*'Prepare Your Own Will: The National Will Kit'* is an exceedingly simple treatment that allows the user to work through the questionnaires, clauses, and checklists toward creation of a valid will. Complex issues involving trusts and guardianships are successfully presented." The only book on self-help wills recommended for legal aid collections.

Library Journal (Special Issue--Collection Development)

"**Highly recommended**. Has been revised and updated to reflect the latest laws; it includes legal forms, questionnaires, and checklists, and everything needed to not only do it yourself, but to understand the ramifications of constructing a will without a lawyer."

Bookwatch

"**A reliable guide** for those wishing to make a simple will. Explains the legal requirements; provides fill-in questionnaires for planning purposes; includes sample clauses, mandatory and optional, arranged in logical order to aid in writing the will; defines legal terminology in a glossary; and includes a state-by-state outline of laws relating to wills. (A) useful addition to public libraries."

Library Journal

"Of all the books mentioned in this review, Sitarz' may be **the easiest to read**. Included are guidelines for the planning and disposition of property and money after death, an overview of probate, step-by-step instructions for preparing the will, personal questionnaires that allows the reader to organize the personal and financial information necessary for wills, a sample will (with explanations of each part), the legal processes involved in signing and safeguarding a will, changes to a will, and an overview of living wills. Worthy of consideration for a collection in any public or academic library serving non-lawyers."

ALA Booklist--Reference Books Bulletin (Special Issue--Law Books for Laypeople)

"**Excellent**. Written by an attorney, with advice valid in all 50 states, this is a blessedly simple guide to writing your own will without entering into the world of high-priced law. There are plenty of sample forms and instructions."

Book Reader

"Sitarz' guide is **a good introduction to the basics of making a will**. The purpose, value, and elements of a will are explained succinctly in non-technical language. The reader is taken through a sample will with the author commenting on the import of various clauses and sections and explaining how to make a will reflect one's intentions. "

Small Press Book Review

Attention:
Computer Users!

Now you can get all of the legal forms in this book on computer diskette with Nova's Forms-on-Disk.

The legal forms in this book and many other Nova Publishing legal books are now available in ASCII format on IBM or MAC disks (3.5" or 5.25"). This allows you to import and modify the forms within your own word processing program. The disks may be used with virtually all common word-processing programs. Nova's Forms-on-Disk gives you computer access to hundreds of award-winning simplified legal forms which are legally-valid in all 50 states and Washington D.C. - the most extensive computer library of personal and small business legal forms available

Ordering Information is contained on the last page of this book.

Prepare Your Own Will:

The National Will Kit

4th Edition

by Daniel Sitarz
Attorney-at-Law

Nova Publishing Company
Small Business and Legal Publications
Carbondale, Illinois

Manufactured in the United States.
Library of Congress Catalog Card Number 94-1325

ISBN 0-935755-128 (Book only) $15.95
ISBN 0-935755-241 (Book with Forms-on-Disk Computer Diskette) $27.95
IBSN 0-935755-225 (Forms-on-Disk Computer Diskette only) $12.95

Library of Congress Cataloging-in-Publication Data
    Sitarz, Dan, 1948-
    Prepare Your Own Will: The National Will Kit / Daniel Sitarz -- Rev. and expand. 4th Edition.
    246 p.   cm. (Legal Self-Help Series) Includes index
    ISBN 0-935755-128 (Book only) $15.95
    ISBN 0-935755-241 (Book with Forms-on-Disk Computer Diskette) $27.95
    IBSN 0-935755-225 (Forms-on-Disk Computer Diskette only) $12.95
    1. Wills--United States--Popular Works 2. Wills--United States--Forms 3. Wills--United States--States--Popular Works I. Sitarz, Dan, 1948-] II. Title III. Series
    KF755.Z9S49   1994   346.7305'4--dc20   [347.30654]   LC94-1325   (pbk)
                                              CIP

Formerly titled: *Prepare Your Last Will and Testament-Without a Lawyer (1st and 2nd Editions)*

Nova Publishing Company is dedicated to providing up-to-date and accurate legal information to the public. All Nova publications are periodically revised to contain the latest available legal information.

4th Edition; 2nd Printing / November, 1995   3rd Edition; 1st Printing / September, 1991
4th Edition; 1st Printing / April, 1994   2nd Edition; 3rd Printing / December, 1990
3rd Edition; 5th Printing / October, 1993   2nd Edition; 2nd Printing / April, 1990
3rd Edition; 4th Printing / January, 1993   2nd Edition; 1st Printing / June, 1989
3rd Edition; 3rd Printing / June, 1992   1st Edition; 2nd Printing / December, 1988
3rd Edition; 2nd Printing / October, 1991   1st Edition; 1st Printing / April, 1988

This publication is designed to provide accurate and authoritative information in regard to the subject matter covered. It is sold with the understanding that the publisher and author are not engaged in rendering legal, accounting, or other professional services. If legal advice or other expert assistance is required, the services of a competent professional person should be sought.

From a Declaration of Principles jointly adopted by a Committee of the American Bar Association and a Committee of Publishers

DISCLAIMER

Nova Publishing Company
Small Business and Consumer Legal Publications
1103 West College Street
Carbondale IL 62901
1(800)748-1175

Distributed to the trade by:
National Book Network
4720 Boston Way
Lanham MD 20706
1(800)462-6420

Table of Contents

Note for computer users: The legal forms in this book and many other Nova Publishing legal books are now available in ASCII format on IBM or MAC disks (3.5" or 5.25"). This allows you to import and modify the forms within your own computer word processing program. The disks may be used with all common word-processing programs. Nova's Forms-on-Disk gives you computer access to hundreds of award-winning simplified legal forms which are legally-valid in all 50 states and Washington D.C. - the most extensive computer library of personal and small business legal forms available to the general public.

Ordering Information is contained on the last page of this book.

Introduction

This book is intended to serve as a guide and explanation of the process and legal procedure required in preparing a valid will without the aid of an attorney. It is part of Nova Publishing Company's continuing series on Legal Self-Help. The various self-help legal guides in this series are prepared by licensed attorneys who feel that public access to the American legal system is long overdue.

With the proper information, the average person in today's world can easily understand and apply many areas of law. Preparing your own will is one of these areas. Understandably, there has been strong resistance by many lawyers against making this type of information available to the public. Many lawyer's jobs depend upon doing things that their clients could do just as well, if the clients simply had access to the proper information and forms. Historically, there have been concerted efforts on the part of the organized Bar and other lawyer organizations to prevent "self-help" legal information, such as is contained in this book, from reaching the general public. These efforts have gone hand-in-hand with an effort to leave the law cloaked in antiquated and unnecessary legal language which, of course, one must pay a lawyer to translate.

Law in American society today is far more pervasive than ever before. There are legal consequences to virtually every public and most private actions in today's world. Leaving knowledge of the law within the hands of only the lawyers in such a society is not only foolish but dangerous as well. A free society depends, in large part, on an informed citizenry. This book and others in Nova's Legal Self-Help Series are intended to provide the necessary information to those members of the public who wish to use and understand the law for themselves.

This book is designed to assist its readers in understanding the general aspects of the law as it relates to wills and after-death distribution of property and to assist its readers in the preparation of their own wills. However, the range of personal finances, property, and desires is infinite and one book can not hope to cover all potential situations or contingencies. In situations involving complex personal or business property holdings, in situations involving complicated or substantial financial investments, or in situations involving unusual or highly-complex post-death distribution plans, readers are advised to seek additional competent legal advice. In addition, estate and inheritance tax laws and regulations are among the most complex laws in existence. Consequently, although a general overview of these laws is provided and the vast majority of people are exempt from Federal estate taxes, readers with very large estates (generally, over $600,000) or complex financial resources are encouraged to seek the assistance of a tax professional if they wish to limit or lessen the tax consequences of the transfer of any property using a will.

Regardless of whether or not a lawyer is ultimately retained in certain situations, the legal information in this handbook will enable the reader to understand the framework of law in this country as it relates to wills. To try and make that task as easy as possible, technical legal jargon has been eliminated whenever possible and plain English used instead. When it is necessary to use a legal term which may be unfamiliar to most people, it will be shown in *italics* and defined when first used. There is a glossary of most legal terms used in wills at the end of this book for your reference in deciphering your current will if it was prepared by an attorney using outdated technical legal language. Lawyers often caution people that such antiquated language is most important and that, of course, only they, the lawyers, can properly prepare and interpret legal documents using such language. Naturally, plain and easily-understood English is not only perfectly proper for use in all legal documents, but in most cases, leads to far less confusion on the part of later readers.

Chapter 1 of this guide will attempt to explain the usefulness and in many cases the necessity of a valid will for insuring that your property and money are passed on to the loved ones that you desire. It will also explain the legal effects of having a will and the potential consequences of not having a will. In Chapter 2 guidelines are provided for planning the distribution of your estate. Your *estate* consists of all of your assets. Other estate planning tools, such as trusts and powers of attorneys, are discussed. In addition, the qualifications necessary for having a will are explained and a step-by-step outline of the procedures to follow to prepare your own will using this book are shown. Chapter 3 provides a discussion of what property may be disposed of using a will and provides a detailed Property Questionnaire which will allow you to assemble the necessary property and financial information which you will need in preparing your will. This chapter also includes information on the inheritance and estate tax consequences of the transfer of property at death. Chapter 4 provides information on who may be a *beneficiary* (one who benefits or receives a gift through a will). This chapter also explains the various forms your gifts may take and also provides a thorough Beneficiary Questionnaire for setting out your decisions on who should receive which of your assets. Chapter 5 includes an overview of information relating to the *probate* (court administration) of your estate, information and a checklist for use by your executor, and a final information sheet for your executor's use in locating your assets and administering your estate.

Fill-in-the-blank will clauses are contained in Chapter 6 for use in preparing your own personally-tailored will. An explanation of each clause and instructions on how to properly fill them in are also provided. The included clauses should be sufficient for most people and most circumstances. In Chapter 7, pre-assembled wills are provided for use if your personal circumstances fit certain standard situations for which they have been prepared. An actual sample will is shown and its various provisions are explained in Chapter 8. The mechanics of actually preparing your will are set forth in Chapter 9. The legal formalities and requirements for signing your will are contained in Chapter 10. These requirements, although not at all difficult, must be followed precisely to insure that your will is acceptable as a valid legal document. Methods and instructions for safeguarding your will are also contained in this chapter.

Chapter 11 contains information regarding when it may be prudent and how to accomplish any changes or alterations to your will at a later date. Chapter 12 provides an explanation and form for your preparation of a *living will*--a document directing that, if you are diagnosed as terminally ill, you desire that no extraordinary life support measures be instituted to artificially prolong your life. In Chapter 13, instructions are provided for preparing a basic *Durable Power of Attorney* form, a document that provides a person of your choosing to have the legal authority to issue instructions to your physician in the event that you are unable to communicate.

The Appendix contains a detailed listing of the individual state legal requirements relating to wills for each of the 50 states and the District of Columbia. Finally, a Glossary of legal terms most often encountered in wills is included.

As with many routine legal tasks, preparation of a will is not as difficult as most people fear. With the proper information before them, most people will be able to prepare a legally valid will which specifically addresses their individual needs in a matter of a few hours. Read through this manual carefully, follow the step-by-step instructions and be assured that your wishes will be safely contained in your own will.

Chapter 1

Why Do You Need A Will?

For most of us, it is very difficult to come to terms with our own mortality. To actually contemplate one's own death is painful. Consequently, very often such thoughts are avoided. However, if you wish to insure that your desires regarding the disposition of your property and possessions after your death are fulfilled, you must confront your mortality and plan accordingly.

Most people's lives are centered on living and, in one way or another, on a close and intimate group of loved ones. These may be relatives, friends, church members, co-workers, or business associates. They are looked to for love, support, and assistance in times of trouble and are asked to share in times of joy. They are often cared about in ways that are difficult to express. But during your life, you at least have the opportunity to show your love and concern in many forms.

It is the purpose of this book to assist you in the difficult task of showing these loved ones your continuing concern for their well-being after you are gone. "You can't take it with you" is a well-worn phrase, but it does strike to the core of the problem of providing for your property and money to be distributed in some fashion on your death. Your entire life has been spent accumulating possessions and wealth for your own comfort and the comfort of your loved ones. Through the proper use of a will, you have a once-in-a-lifetime opportunity to personally decide what will happen to your accumulated wealth and possessions when you are gone. It is your entirely personal decision. Indeed, it is your legal privilege to make this decision. No one but you has the power to decide, prior to your death, how and to whom your property should be distributed on your demise. But to do so, you must take the initiative and overcome the understandable difficulty of these decisions. If you do not take the initiative and prepare your own will, on your death an impersonal court will decide who will receive your wealth.

To actually sit down and decide how your property and possessions should be divided amongst your loved ones in the event of your own death is not an easy task. However, it is you alone who knows your wishes. The property and possessions that you own may be land, your home, your personal household furnishings, keepsakes, heirlooms, money, stocks, bonds, or any other type of property. It may be worth thousands of dollars or it may be worth far less. If you are like most people, you want to insure that it is passed on to the persons whom you choose. But again, if you are like most people, you have put off making a will. Nearly 75% of Americans are without a valid will.

A *will* is a legal document that, when accepted by the probate court, is proof of an intent to transfer property to the persons or organizations named in the will upon the death of the maker of the will. The maker of the will is known as the *testator*. A will is effective for the transfer of property that is owned by the testator on the date of his death. A will can be changed, modified, or revoked at any time by the testator prior to death.

It is equally important to understand that for a will to be valid, it must generally be prepared, witnessed, and signed according to certain technical legal procedures. Although a will is perfectly valid if it is written in plain English and does not use technical legal language, it **must** be prepared, witnessed, and signed in the manner outlined in this book. This can not be overemphasized. You can not take any shortcuts when following the instructions as they relate to the procedures necessary for completing and signing your will. These procedures are not at all difficult and consist generally of carefully typing your will in the manner outlined later, signing it in the manner specified, and having three witnesses and a notary public also sign the document. (Although not a legal requirement, the notarization of your will can aid in its proof in court later, if necessary). [Note: Louisiana residents must follow the procedures noted at the end of Chapter 10].

In the past, it was in many cases possible to simply write down your wishes, sign the paper, and be confident that your wishes would be followed upon your death. Unfortunately, this is, in most cases, no longer possible. *Holographic* (or handwritten and unwitnessed) wills are no longer accepted as valid in most jurisdictions. *Nuncupative* (or oral) wills are also not admissible in most probate courts to prove a person's intent to dispose of property on death. For this reason, a valid, typewritten will which is prepared, signed, and witnessed according to formal legal requirements is now essentially the only secure method to assure the desired disposition of your property, possessions, and money after your death and to assure that your loved ones are taken care of according to your final wishes.

In some cases (for example, those involving extremely complicated business or personal financial holdings or the desire to create a complex trust arrangement) it is clearly advisable to consult an attorney for the preparation of your will. However, in most circumstances and for most people, the terms of a will which can provide for the necessary protection are relatively routine and may safely be prepared without the added expense of consulting a lawyer.

Reasons For Having A Will

There are many reasons why it is desirable to have a will. Perhaps most important is to insure that it is *you* who decides how your estate is distributed on your death and to be assured that those loved ones whom you wish to share in your bounty actually receive your gifts.

To Avoid Having the State Decide Who Will Receive Your Property

What happens to your property and possessions if you do not have a valid and legal will or if the will that you have is found by the probate court to be invalid because it was not signed or witnessed properly? Law books are filled with many unfortunate cases in which, because of the lack of a formal and valid will, the true desires and wishes of a person as to who should inherit their property have been frustrated. If there is no valid will to use for direction, a probate judge must give a person's property to either the spouse, children, or the closest blood relatives of the deceased person. This result is required even in situations when it is perfectly clear that the deceased person did not, under any circumstances, want those relatives to inherit the property. Although the probate judge is required to interpret a will to best satisfy what appears to be the written intentions of the person who signed it, the judge must first have before him a valid will.

To be valid, the document must, generally, have been signed and witnessed in a formal manner and prepared in such a way as to satisfy certain legal requirements. These requirements are strictly enforced to ensure that the document presented to a probate court is, indeed, the real and valid will of the deceased person whose property is to be divided.

Without such a valid will before him or her, a judge must rely on a legislative scheme which has been devised to make for an orderly distribution of property in all cases where there is no valid will. This scheme is present as law, in one form or another, in all 50 states and is generally referred to as *intestate distribution*.

The terms of state intestate distribution plans are very complex in most states. In general, a person's spouse is first in line to receive the property when there is no will at death. Most states provide that the spouse and children will either share the entire estate or the surviving spouse will take it all in the hopes that the spouse will share it with the children. Generally, the spouse will receive one-half and the children will receive one-half.

In many states, if a person dies without a valid will and is survived by a spouse but not by any children, the spouse will inherit the entire estate and the surviving parents, brother, sisters and any other blood relatives to the deceased will be entitled to nothing.

If there is no surviving spouse or children, the blood relatives of the deceased will receive the estate. If there is someone or several persons within the next closest relationship level (for example, parents or brothers or sisters) who is alive on the death of the person, then these relatives will receive all of the person's property or share it equally with all others alive that are in a similar relationship level. Once a level of blood relationship is found in which there is at least one living person, all persons who are more distantly related inherit nothing.

In addition, these legislative distribution plans are set up on the assumption that family members are the only parties that a deceased person would wish to have inherit his or her property. Thus, without a will, it is impossible to leave any gifts to close friends, in-laws, blood relatives more distant then any alive, charities, or organizations of any type. If there is no will and if there are no blood relatives alive, the state confiscates all of a person's property under a legal doctrine entitled *escheat*.

As an example of a typical legislative intestate distribution scheme, the following is a general representative outline of the various levels of distribution that are set up in many states. Keep in mind, however, that this example is only an illustration of the method that states may use and is not intended to be used in determining how your own estate would be divided. Check on the listing in the Appendix for your own state's intestate distribution plan for specific details:

- If a spouse and children of the spouse are surviving: $50,000 and 1/2 of balance of the estate will go to the spouse and 1/2 of balance of the estate will go to the children equally. If one of the children has predeceased the parent and leaves surviving children (grandchildren of the deceased parent), then the grandchildren will split the deceased child's share.

- If a spouse and children not of spouse are surviving: 1/2 of balance of the estate will go to the spouse and 1/2 of balance of the estate will go to the children equally. If one of the children has predeceased the parent and leaves surviving children (grandchildren of the deceased parent), then the grandchildren will split the deceased child's share.

- If a spouse, but no children or parents of the deceased are surviving: All of the estate will go to the spouse.

- If a spouse and one or both parents, but no children are surviving: $50,000 and 1/2 of balance of the estate will go to the spouse and 1/2 of balance of the estate will go to the parents equally. If only one parent is surviving, that parent gets the entire 1/2 share of the estate.

- If there are children of the deceased, but no spouse surviving: All of the estate goes to the children. If one of the children has predeceased the parent and leaves surviving children (grandchildren of the deceased parent), then the grandchildren will split the deceased child's share.

- If one or both parents, but no spouse or children are surviving: All of the estate will go to the parents equally, or the entire estate will go to the surviving parent.

- If there is no spouse, no children, or no parents surviving: All of the estate will go to brothers and sisters equally. If a brother or sister has predeceased the deceased sibling and has left surviving children, their children will split the deceased brother or sister's share.

- If there is no spouse, no children, no parents, and no brothers and sisters or their children surviving: 1/2 of the estate will go to the maternal grandparents and 1/2 will go to the paternal grandparents. If the grandparents on either side have predeceased the decedent, their children will split their share.

- If there is no spouse, no children, no parents, and no brothers and sisters or their children, and no grandparents or their children surviving: The estate will pass to the surviving members of the closest level of blood relatives: aunts, uncles, nephews, nieces, great-grandparents, great uncles, great aunts, first cousins, great-great grandparents, second cousins, etc.

- If there are no surviving kin: The estate will be claimed by the state under the doctrine of escheat.

Many disastrous consequences can result from having your property distributed according to a standardized state plan. Take, for example, a situation in which a person and his or her spouse die from injuries sustained in a single accident, but one spouse survives a few hours longer. If there is no will, the result in this scenario is that the property of the first one to die passes to the spouse who survives. A few hours later, on the death of the surviving spouse, the property automatically passes only to the relatives of the spouse who survived the longest. The relatives of the first to die can inherit nothing at all. This, obviously would not normally be the desired consequence. Under the typical state scheme, luck and chance play a large role in deciding who is to inherit property.

Each state has a complicated and often different method for deciding which particular family members will take property when there is no will. However, the results are often far from the desires of how the person actually wished to have the property distributed. Obviously, under this type of state distribution of your property, the individual circumstances of your family are not taken into consideration at all nor are any intentions that you may have had, regardless of how strongly you may have expressed them during your lifetime. The only way to avoid having the state decide who is to receive your property is to have prepared a legally valid will. If you die without a valid will, the state essentially writes one for you on its own terms.

To Appoint an Executor Who Will Administer Your Property

Another very important reason for having a will is the ability to appoint an executor of your own choice. An *executor* is your personal representative for seeing that your wishes, as contained in your will, are carried out after your death and that your taxes and debts are paid. An executor also collects and inventories all of your property and is in charge of seeing that it is distributed according to your wishes as expressed in your will.

Typically, a spouse or a brother or sister, or other close family member or trusted friend is chosen to act as executor. However, it may be any responsible adult that you would feel confident having this duty. It may even be a local bank or trust company. In that case, of course, there will be an often substantial fee charged to your estate for the completion of these generally routine duties by the corporate executor. If you choose an individual, he or she should be a resident of your home state. The will clauses in Chapter 6 or a pre-assembled will in Chapter 7 will enable you to appoint your executor and an alternate executor so that, in the event your first choice can not perform, it is still your personal choice as to who will administer your will.

If you do not have a will or if you do not choose an executor in your will, the probate court judge will appoint someone to administer the distribution of your property. Often it will be a local attorney, court official, or bank officer who may not know you or your beneficiaries at all. Your estate will then be distributed by a stranger who will charge your estate a hefty fee for the collection and distribution of your assets.

By appointing your own executor, you are also able to waive the posting of a bond by your executor and, most often, a family member executor will not accept a fee for serving. This will allow more of your assets to reach your beneficiaries, rather than paying for the expenses of administration of your estate.

To Appoint a Guardian for Your Minor Children

For those with minor children, the appointment of a guardian for any children is another very important item which may be accomplished through the use of a will. A *guardian "of the person"*, as this type of guardian is usually referred to, is responsible for the actual care, custody, and upbringing of a child. If your spouse is alive, he or she would generally be appointed as guardian in any event, with or without a will. However, there is the possibility that you both will be killed in a single accident or catastrophe. Also, if you are a single parent, you will need to designate a choice for guardian. Without a will for direction, a probate judge has little guidance in choosing the person whom you feel would be the best alternative for caring for your children. With a will, however, you can select a guardian for just such an eventuality.

To Appoint a Guardian or Trustee to Administer Property for a Child

You can also have such a guardian administer the property or money which you leave to your children (a *guardian "of the property"*), or you may set up a trust and appoint a trustee to administer your children's inheritance until a time when you feel that they will be able to handle their own affairs. A *trust* consists of assets which are managed and distributed by a *trustee* to benefit one or more *beneficiaries*. Instructions to provide for these alternatives are simply stated in a will, but are more difficult to accomplish without one. If such is not provided for in a will, and a minor child is left money or property by way of the state intestate succession laws, the courts will generally decide who should administer the property. Such court-supervised guardianship of the property or money will automatically end at the child's reaching the legal age of majority in the state (usually 18 years of age). At this age, without a will to direct otherwise, the child will receive full control over the property and/or money. This may not be the most prudent result, as many 18 year-olds are not capable of managing property or large sums of money. With a will, it is easy to arrange for the property or money to be held in trust and used to benefit the child until a later age, perhaps 21, 25, or even 30 years of age.

To Disinherit a Child or Other Relative

Disinheritance of a child or other relative whom you feel is not deserving of your property, or has no need of your property, is also something that can be accomplished only through the use of a will. Although the total disinheritance of a spouse is not possible under the laws of any state, any other relative may, generally, be cut off without a penny from your estate through the use of a will. [Note: In Louisiana, neither a spouse nor children may be totally disinherited.]

To Accomplish Other Results

Many other things may be accomplished only through the use of a will. You can forgive a debt which is owed to you in your will. You can revoke any other previous wills. You can provide instructions for organ donations, the disposition of your body, and burial, although it is generally wise to also leave these instructions with your executor on a separate sheet. Additionally, the proper use of a will normally lessens the expenses of probate, since the disposition of all of your property has been planned in advance, by you.

Even if you have used the various estate planning tools outlined in the next chapter to attempt to have your estate avoid probate, a will is still highly recommended. There may be assets that you have neglected, forgotten about, or will not be uncovered until your death. If you have used a trust, joint property agreements, and other estate planning tools, these unknown or forgotten assets may wind up passing to your heirs as intestate property and causing probate proceedings to be instituted. Through the use of a simple will, you can avoid this possibility.

Although it can be short and simple, a will is an important document which can accomplish many tasks. The proper use of a will can eliminate much confusion for those left behind. As it provides a clear and legal record of your wishes, it can avoid feuding and squabbles among your family members. Perhaps most importantly, it can make your last wishes come true.

Chapter 2

Planning Your Will

A will is the cornerstone of any comprehensive arrangement to plan for the distribution of your property upon your death. In this chapter, the basic qualifications for having a will are outlined. Various other estate planning tools which may be useful in certain situations are also detailed. Finally, an overview of the steps you will take in preparing your own will is presented.

Qualifications for Having a Will

Are you legally qualified to have a will? In general, if you are over 18 years of age and of "sound mind", you will qualify. There are a few states which have different minimum ages, some allowing wills by children as young as 14, and a few requiring the testator to be over 18. For the specific age requirements, check your own state's age requirements in the Appendix.

It is also important to understand that laws of different states may apply to a single will. The laws of the state in which you have your principal residence will be used to decide the validity of the will as to any personal property and real estate located in that state. However, if any real estate outside of your home state is mentioned in the will, then the laws of the state in which that real estate is found will govern the disposition of that particular real estate. Thus, if you own property outside of the state where you live, when you check the Appendix for information concerning specific state laws, be certain to check both your own state's laws and those of the state in which your other property is located.

The requirement to have a "sound mind" refers to the ability to understand the following:

- That you are signing a will,
- That you know who your beneficiaries are,
- That you understand the nature and extent of your assets.

Having a "sound mind" refers only to the moment when you actually *execute* (sign) the will. A person who is suffering from a mental illness, or a person who uses drugs or alcohol, or even a person who is senile may legally sign a will. This is acceptable as long as the will is signed and understood during a period when the person is lucid and has sufficient mental ability to understand the extent of his or her property, who is to receive that property, and that it is a will that is being signed.

The fact that a person has a physical incapacity makes no difference in their right to sign a will. Regardless if a person is blind, deaf, can not speak, is very physically weak, or is illiterate; as long as they understand what it is they are doing and what they are signing, the "sound mind" requirement is met.

Related to the requirement that the testator have a "sound mind" at the time of signing the will is the requirement that the will be signed without any undue influence, fraud, or domination by others. In other words, the will must be freely signed and reflect the wishes of the person signing it for it to be legally valid. You do not ever have to sign a will that is not exactly what you desire. Do not let anyone coerce or force you to sign a will that does not accurately reflect your own personal wishes. If you are in a situation of this nature, it is highly recommended that you immediately seek the assistance of a competent lawyer.

Other Estate Planning Tools

The use of a will is, by far, the most popular and widespread legal tool for planning for the distribution of your estate. Your *estate* consists of everything that you own, whether it is real estate or personal property. As explained in Chapter 1, through the use of a will you can accomplish the planned distribution of your estate property and many other goals. However, there may be other objectives in your planning that can not be accomplished solely through the use of a will. Other estate planning documents may be necessary to achieve all of your goals.

There are three basic reasons that other estate planning tools may be useful in certain situations: avoidance of probate, reducing taxes, and health care considerations.

First, many people desire to avoid having their property be subject to probate proceedings. Although in some situations, the probate process has been abused, there are valid reasons for allowing your property to be handled through probate. It allows for an examination of the validity of your will. It provides a process by which the improper distribution of your assets is guarded against. Having your property distributed through a probate process also puts a definite limit on the length of time that a creditor can file a claim against your estate.

The drawbacks of probate are that it can delay the distribution of your property while the probate process continues. The probate of an estate can take, generally, from 4 to 18 months, and sometimes much longer. Additionally, probate costs can be substantial. Court costs, appraisal fees, lawyer's fees, and accounting bills can all cut deeply into the amount of property and funds that will eventually be distributed to your beneficiaries. However, for small estates (generally, under $100,000) most states have simplified probate procedures which can be handled without lawyers and can substantially reduce these costs. The probate process itself is explained in more detail in Chapter 5.

There are various methods for avoiding having property pass to others through the probate process. The four most important are as follows:

- **Joint tenancy with right of survivorship**
  Upon one owner's death, any property held as *joint tenants with right of survivorship* passes automatically to the surviving owner without probate or court intervention of any kind. Under the laws of most states, the description of ownership on the deed or other title document must specifically state that the property is being held by the people as "joint tenants with right of survivorship". If not, the property is usually presumed to be held as "*tenants-in-common*", which means that each owner owns a certain specific share of the property which they may leave by way of a will or other estate planning device. Some states have another class of property known as "*tenancy-by-the-entirety*" which is, essentially, a joint tenancy specifically for spouses. More information on property ownership is provided in Chapter 3.

- **Living or revocable trusts**
  An increasingly popular estate planning tool, living or revocable trusts can be effectively used to avoid probate. This type of document generally provides that all or most of a person's property be transferred to trust ownership. The owner of the property generally retains full control and management of the trust as *trustee*. In the trust document, beneficiaries are chosen, much the same as in a will. The terms of the trust can actually parallel the terms of a will. The difference is that, upon the death of the creator (*trustor*) of the trust, all of the property that has been transferred to trust ownership passes immediately and automatically to the beneficiaries without any court intervention or supervision.

The owner of the property retains full control over the property until death and the creator of the trust can terminate this type of trust at any time prior to death. However, there are increased paperwork requirements in setting up and operating a trust. The trust itself must be prepared and all of your property ownership (stocks, bonds, bank accounts, real estate deeds, car titles, etc.) actually transferred to the trust. For information regarding the use and preparation of living trusts, please see: *"The Complete Book of Personal Legal Forms"* by Daniel Sitarz (Nova Publishing Company, 1993).

- ### *Life insurance*
  Another common method of passing funds to a person on death while avoiding probate is through the use of life insurance. By making the premium payments throughout your life, you are accumulating assets for distribution on your death. The life insurance benefits are paid directly to your chosen beneficiaries without probate court intervention. However, life insurance benefits are still considered part of your taxable estate. For more information on insurance, you are advised to consult an insurance professional.

- ### *Payable-on-death bank accounts*
  This type of property ownership consists of a bank account held in trust for a named beneficiary. It may also be referred to as a "Totten" trust or a "Bank" trust account. It is a very simple method for providing that the assets in a bank account are paid immediately to a beneficiary on your death without the beneficiary having any control over the account during your life, as is the case with a joint bank account. This trust-type bank account allows for the property to be transferred without probate and is very simple to set up. Any type of bank account, whether checking, savings, money market, or even certificates of deposit, may be designated as a payable-on-death account by filling out simple forms at your financial institution.

The second major use for estate planning tools is to attempt to lessen or completely avoid the payment of any taxes on the transfer of property upon death. Upon death, the transfer of property may be subject to federal estate taxes, state estate taxes, and state inheritance taxes. However, much of the taxation of estates (most importantly, federal taxation) does not become a factor unless your estate is valued at over $600,000. Thus, for most people, the need to pursue complicated tax avoidance estate plans is unnecessary. For reference, however, details regarding taxation of estates are provided in Chapter 3. In addition, the Appendix contains information regarding each individual state's laws on gift, inheritance, and estate taxation. The complexity of tax laws and of the methods to avoid taxes through estate planning is beyond the scope of this book. If your estate is over $600,000, it may be wise to seek the assistance of a tax professional.

The third main purpose of estate planning is a relatively new concern. Recent advances in medical technology have allowed modern medicine, in many cases, to significantly extend the lives of many people. In addition, many people have become aware of the possibility of their lives being continued indefinitely through technological life support procedures. Two legal documents have been developed to deal with these concerns.

● **_Living will_**

A living will is a document that can be used to state your desire that extraordinary life support means not be used to artificially prolong your life in the event that you are stricken with a terminal disease or injury. Its use has been recognized in the vast majority of states in recent years. The Appendix provides information regarding the recognition of living wills in each state. Chapter 12 explains the use of the document in detail and provides the necessary forms and instructions for preparation of a living will.

● **_Durable power of attorney_**

This relatively new legal document has been developed to allow a person to appoint another person to handle all of their affairs in the event that they become incapacitated or incompetent. Generally, this document will only take effect upon a person becoming unable to manage their own affairs. In addition, this type of document may be used to delegate the legal authority to make health care decisions to another person. This document may be carefully tailored to fit your needs and concerns and may be used in conjunction with a living will. It can be a valuable tool for dealing with difficult health care situations. Instructions and forms for preparing a basic durable power of attorney are included in Chapter 13.

This book provides the information necessary to prepare the three basic legal documents in estate planning: a will, a living will, and a durable power of attorney. Regardless of what other types of estate planning tools you eventually decide are appropriate in your situation, these two basic documents are necessary complements to any successful estate plan. If you believe that your situation warrants additional estate planning, please consult an experienced financial planner, tax professional, or attorney. You may, of course, also wish to research and prepare any of the above documents yourself without the aid of an attorney or accountant. There are many estate planning books available. Check your public or local law library.

Steps in Preparing Your Will

There are several steps that must be followed to properly prepare your will using this book. None of them are very difficult or overly complicated. However, they must be done carefully in order to effectively accomplish what you set out to do: be assured that your property is left to those loved ones that you choose and that your loved ones are properly cared for after your death.

What follows is a brief outline of the necessary steps which must be followed to prepare a valid will with this book. You will probably refer back to this chapter several times in the course of preparing your own will to be certain that you are on the right track and have not left out any steps.

The following steps are numbered 1 through 10 for your ease in following them:

1. Read through this entire book. You are advised to read carefully through this entire book before you actually begin preparing your own will. By doing this you will gain an overview of the entire process and will have a much better idea of where you are heading before you actually begin the preparation of your will.

2. Fill in the Property Questionnaire contained in Chapter 3 and the Beneficiary Questionnaire in Chapter 4. These questionnaires are designed to compile all of the necessary personal information for your will preparation. Information regarding your personal and business assets, percentages of ownership of these assets, marital relationship, names and addresses of relatives, and many other items will be gathered together in these questionnaires for your use. As you fill in these questionnaires, you will be making the actual decisions regarding distribution of your assets. In addition, in Chapter 5, you will fill out an Executor Information List which will provide important data for use by your chosen executor.

3. Review your own state's legal requirements as contained in the Appendix. The Appendix contains a concise listing of the laws relating to wills in every state. Although the standard will clauses used in this book will alleviate most of the concerns raised by these legal requirements, there may be certain of your own state's requirements which will affect how you decide to prepare your own will.

4. This book contains two methods by which to prepare a will: (1) by choosing individual will clauses from Chapter 6 and assembling your own custom-tailored will or (2) by filling in the blanks of pre-assembled wills contained in Chapter 7. Read through all of the will clauses and pre-assembled wills and decide which clauses or complete will most clearly fits your needs. This is one of the most important steps in the process and one which must be done very carefully. The various clauses and wills are, for the most part, self-explanatory and you should be able to

easily decide which ones apply to your situation. However, you are advised to read through each and every clause before you decide on the final choices for your own will.

5.   Make a photo-copy of all of those portions of Chapter 6 or Chapter 7 which will be included in your own will, including any mandatory clauses as noted. These photo-copies will be your will preparation worksheets. After you have done this, fill in the appropriate information on the photo-copies using your Property and Beneficiary Questionnaires. When your worksheets have been completely filled-in, number each included will clause consecutively beginning with #1.

6.   Type a clean original of your will as explained in Chapter 9. With your filled-in photo-copy worksheet before you, this should be a relatively easy task of simply copying the provisions which you have selected.

7.   Proofread your entire will very carefully to be certain that it is exactly what you want. If there are any typographical errors or if you want to change some provision, no matter how slight, you **must** retype that page of your will. **Do not** make any corrections on the will itself.

8.   Assemble your witnesses and notary public and formally sign your will. This is known as the *execution* of your will and must be done very carefully following the details contained in Chapter 10.

9.   Make a photo-copy of your original, signed will and give it to the executor that you have named in your will. You may also wish to give the executor a copy of the Executor Information List from Chapter 5. Store the original of your will in a safe place as outlined in Chapter 10.

10.   Review your will periodically and prepare a new will or *codicil* (a formally-executed change to a will) if necessary as detailed in Chapter 11.

That's all there is to it. Actually, that may sound like a lot of work and bother, but realize that you would have to follow many of the same steps even if a lawyer were to prepare your will. However, in that case, you would give him or her all of the information and he or she would simply prepare a will in much the same fashion that you will use in this book. The difference, of course, is that you must pay an often exorbitant price to have this done by a lawyer. Additionally, by preparing your will yourself and doing so at your own pace, you are certain to take more care and give more thought to the entire process than if you have someone else prepare it for you.

The following is a quick checklist of the 10 steps noted above:

- ❑ Read this entire book first.
- ❑ Fill in the Property and Beneficiary Questionnaires.
- ❑ Review your state's legal requirements.
- ❑ Choose the appropriate will clauses or pre-assembled will.
- ❑ Make a photo-copy rough-draft version of your will and fill it in.
- ❑ Type an original of your will.
- ❑ Carefully proofread your will.
- ❑ Assemble the witnesses and notary public and sign your will.
- ❑ Give a copy of your will to your executor and store the original in a safe place.
- ❑ Review your will periodically and make any changes in a formal manner.

Chapter 3

Property Questionnaire

The methods and manners of disposition of your property using a will are discussed in this chapter. Your assets consist of different types of property. It may be personal property, real estate, "community" property, stocks, bonds, cash, heirlooms, or keepsakes. Regardless of the type of property you own, there are certain general rules which must be kept in mind as you prepare your will.

In addition, in this chapter you will prepare an inventory of all of your assets and liabilities. This will allow you to have before you a complete listing of all of the property that you own as you begin to consider which beneficiaries should receive which property.

What property may you dispose of with your will?

In general, you may dispose of any property that you own at the time of your death. This simple fact, however, contains certain factors which require further explanation. There are forms of property which you may "own", but which may not be transferred by way of a will. In addition, you may own only a percentage or share of certain other property. In such situations, only that share or percentage which you actually own may be left by your will. Finally, there are types of property ownership which are automatically transferred to another party at your death, regardless of the presence of a will.

In the first category of property which can ***not*** be transferred by will are properties which have a designated beneficiary outside of the provisions of your will. These types of properties include:

☒   Life insurance policies;
☒   Retirement plans;
☒   IRA's and KEOGH's;
☒   Pension plans;
☒   Trust bank accounts;
☒   Living trust assets;
☒   Payable-on-death bank accounts;
☒   U.S. Savings Bonds, with payable-on-death beneficiaries.

In general, if there is already a valid determination of who will receive the property upon your death (as there is, for example, in the choice of a life insurance beneficiary), you may not alter this choice of beneficiary through the use of your will. If you wish to alter your choice of beneficiary in any of these cases, please directly alter the choice with the holder of the particular property (for instance, the life insurance company or bank).

The next category of property which may have certain restrictions regarding its transfer by will is property in which you may only own a certain share or percentage. Examples of this may be a partnership interest in a company or jointly-held property. Using a will, you may only leave that percentage or fraction of the ownership of the property that is actually yours. For business interests, it is generally advisable to pass the interest which you own to a beneficiary intact. The forced sale of the share of a business for estate distribution purposes often results in a lower value being placed on the share. Of course, certain partnership and other business ownership agreements require the sale of a partner's or owner's interest upon death. These buy-out provisions will be contained in any ownership or partnership documents that you may have. Review such documentation carefully to determine both the exact share of your ownership and any post-death arrangements.

The ownership rights and shares of property owned jointly must be considered. This is discussed below under *common law* property states, although most joint ownership laws also apply in *community property* states as well. Another example of property in which only a certain share is actually able to be transferred by will is a spouse's share of marital property in states which follow community property designation of certain jointly owned property. The following is a discussion of the basic property law rules in both community property and common law property states. The rules regarding community property only apply to married persons in those states that follow this type of property designation. If you are single, please disregard this section and use the common law property states rules below to determine your ownership rights.

Community Property states

Several states, mostly in the Western United States, follow the *community property* type of marital property system. Please refer to the Appendix to see if your state has this type of system. The system itself is derived from ancient Spanish law. It is a relatively simple concept. All property owned by either spouse during a marriage is divided into two types: separate property and community property.

Separate property consists of all property considered owned entirely by one spouse. Separate property, essentially, is all property owned by the spouse prior to the marriage and kept separate during the marriage; and all property received individually by the spouse by gift or inheritance during the marriage. All other property is considered *community* property. In other words, all property acquired during the marriage by either spouse, unless by gift or inheritance, is community property. Community property is considered to be owned in equal shares by each spouse, regardless of whose efforts actually went into acquiring the property. (One major exception to this general rule is Social Security and Railroad retirement benefits, which are considered to be separate property by Federal law).

Specifically, separate property generally consists of:

●   All property owned by a spouse prior to a marriage (if kept separate);

●   All property a spouse receives by gift or inheritance during a marriage (if kept separate);

●   All income derived from separate property (if kept separate) [Except in Texas and Idaho where income from separate property is considered community property].

Community property generally consists of:

●   All property acquired by either spouse during the course of a marriage, unless it is separate property (thus it is community property unless acquired by gift or inheritance or is income from separate property);

●   All pensions and retirement benefits earned during a marriage (except Social Security and Railroad retirement benefits);

●   All employment income of either spouse acquired during the marriage;

●   All separate property which is mixed or co-mingled with community property during the marriage.

Thus, if you are a married resident of a community property state, the property which you may dispose of by will consists of all of your separate property and one-half of your jointly-owned marital community property. The other half of the community property automatically becomes your spouse's sole property on your death.

Residents of community property states may also own property jointly as tenant-in-common or as joint tenants. These forms of property ownership are discussed below.

Common Law Property states

Residents of all other states are governed by a *common law* property system, which was derived from English law. Under this system, there is no rule which gives fifty percent ownership of the property acquired during marriage to each spouse.

In common law states, the property which you may dispose of with your will consists of all the property held by title in your name, any property which you have earned or purchased with your own money, and any property which you may have been given as a gift or inherited, either before or during your marriage.

If your name alone is on a title document in these states (for instance, a deed or automobile title), then you own it solely. If your name and your spouse's name is on the document, you generally own it as *tenant's-in-common*, unless it specifically states that your ownership is to be as *joint tenants* or if your state allows for a *tenancy-by-the-entireties* (a form of joint tenancy between married persons). There is an important difference between these types of joint ownership: namely, survivorship.

With property owned as tenants-in-common, the percentage or fraction that each tenant-in-common owns is property which may be disposed of under a will. If the property is held as joint tenants or as tenants-by-the entireties, the survivor automatically receives the deceased party's share. Thus, in your will, you may not dispose of any property held in joint tenancy or tenancy-by-the entirety since it already has an automatic legal disposition upon your death. For example: if two persons own a parcel of real estate as equal tenants-in-common, each person may leave a 1/2 interest in the property to the beneficiary of their choice by their will. By contrast, if the property is owned as joint tenants with right of survivorship, the 1/2 interest that a person owns will automatically become the surviving owner's property upon death.

In common-law states, you may dispose of any property which has your name on the title in whatever share that the title gives you, unless the title is held specifically as joint tenants or tenants-by-the entireties. You may also dispose of any property which you earned or purchased with your own money, and any property which you have been given as a gift or inherited. If you are married, however, there is a further restriction on your right to dispose of property by will.

All common law states protect spouses from total disinheritance by providing a statutory scheme under which a spouse may choose to take a minimum share of the deceased spouse's estate, regardless of what the will states. This effectively prevents any spouse from being entirely disinherited through the use of the common law rules of property (name on the title = ownership of property).

In most states, the spouse has a right to a one-third share of the deceased spouse's estate, regardless of what the deceased spouse's will states. However, all states are slightly different in how they apply this type of law and some allow a spouse to take up to one-half of the estate. Please check your particular state's laws on this aspect in the Appendix. The effect of these statutory provisions is to make it impossible to disinherit a spouse entirely. If you choose to leave nothing to your spouse under your will or by other means (such as life insurance or joint tenancies), he or she may take it anyway, generally from any property which you tried to leave to others. The details of each state's spousal statutory share are outlined in the Appendix.

Some states also allow a certain *family allowance* or *homestead allowance* to the spouse or children to insure that they are not abruptly cut off from their support by any terms of a will. These allowances are generally of short duration and for relatively minor amounts of money and differ greatly from state to state.

Thus, the property which you may dispose of by will is as follows:

❑   In all states: Your share of any of the following property, except property for which a beneficiary has been chosen by the terms of the ownership of the property itself (for example: life insurance or living trusts).

❑   In community property states: All separate property (property which was brought into a marriage, or obtained by gift or inheritance during the marriage) and one-half of the community property (all other property acquired during the marriage by either spouse). If you are single, follow the common law rules below.

❑   In common law states: Your share of all property in which your name is on the title document, unless it is held as joint tenants or tenants-by-the-entireties and your share of all other property which you own, earned, or purchased in your own name. Please check the Appendix for information relating to the spouse's minimum statutory share of an estate.

Federal Estate Taxes and State Inheritance and Estate Taxes

Various taxes may apply to property transfers upon death. In general, there are two main type of taxes: estate taxes and inheritance taxes. An estate tax is a government tax on the privilege of being allowed to transfer property on to others upon your death. This tax is assessed against the estate itself and is paid out of the estate before the assets are distributed to the beneficiaries. An inheritance tax is a tax on property received and is paid by the person who has actually inherited the property. The federal government assesses an estate tax. Various states impose additional estate taxes and inheritance taxes. Additionally, the federal government and a few states apply a gift tax on property transfers during a person's life. Nevada is the only state which does not impose any estate, inheritance, or gift taxes. Basic information regarding each state's tax situation is provided in the Appendix.

With regard to estate taxes, recent changes in the federal Income Tax Code, as it relates to estate taxes, have released an estimated 95% of the American public from any federal estate tax liability on their death. The current IRS rules provide for the equivalent of an exemption from all estate tax for the first $600,000 of a person's assets. In addition, all of the value of a person's estate that is left to a spouse is exempt from any federal estate tax. Even if your particular assets are over this minimum exemption, there are still methods to lessen or eliminate your tax liability. These methods, however, are beyond the scope of this book. Therefore, if your assets (or your joint assets, if married) total over approximately $600,000, it is recommended that you consult a tax professional prior to preparing your will.

State estate taxes are, as a rule, also very minimal or even non-existent until the value of your estate is over $600,000. Most state's estate tax laws are tied directly to the federal estate tax regulations and thus allow for the same level of exemption equivalent from state estate taxes on death if the estate property totals under $600,000. A few states may impose an additional level of estate tax. The details of each state's estate tax situation are outlined in the Appendix.

Less than half of the states impose an inheritance tax on the receipt of property resulting from the death of another. There are generally relatively high exemptions allowed and the inheritance taxes are usually scaled such that spouses, children, and close relatives pay much lower rates than more distant relatives or unrelated persons.

From a planning standpoint, the changes in the federal estate tax have virtually eliminated any consideration of tax consequences from the preparation of a will for most Americans. Other factors, however, will affect the planning of your will.

Property Questionnaire

Before you begin to actually prepare your own will, you must understand what your assets are, who your beneficiaries are to be, and what your personal desires are as to how those assets should be distributed among your beneficiaries.

Since you may only give away property which you actually own, before you prepare your will it is helpful to gather all of the information regarding your personal financial situation together in one place. The following Property Questionnaire will assist you in that task.

Determining who your dependents are, what their financial circumstances are, what gifts you wish to leave them, and whether you wish to make other persons or organizations beneficiaries under your will are questions that will be answered as you complete the Beneficiary Questionnaire in Chapter 4.

Together, these two Questionnaires should provide you with all of the necessary information to make the actual preparation of your will a relatively easy task. In addition, the actual process of filling out these questions will gently force you to think about and make the important decisions which must be made in the planning and preparation of your will.

When you have finished completing this Questionnaire, have it before you as you select and fill in your personal will clauses in Chapter 6 or 7.

It may also be prudent to leave a photo-copy of these Questionnaires with the original of your will and provide a copy to your executor, in order to provide a readily-accessible inventory of your assets and list of your beneficiaries for use by your executor in managing your estate.

Property Questionnaire

What are your assets?

Cash and bank accounts

(Individual accounts can be left by will; jointly tenancy and payable-on-death accounts can not.)

Checking Account .... $ _____
Bank _____
Account # _____
Name(s) on account _____

Checking Account .... $ _____
Bank _____
Account # _____
Name(s) on account _____

Savings Account .... $ _____
Bank _____
Account # _____
Name(s) on account _____

Savings Account .... $ _____
Bank _____
Account # _____
Name(s) on account _____

Certificate of Deposit .... $ _____
Held by _____
Expiration date _____
Name(s) on account _____

Other Account .... $ _____
Bank _____
Account # _____
Name(s) on account _____

Total Cash .... $ _____

Life insurance and annuity contracts

(Life insurance benefits can not be left by will.)

Ordinary Life .... $ _____
Company _____
Policy # _____
Beneficiary _____
Address _____

Ordinary Life .... $ _____
Company _____
Policy # _____
Beneficiary _____
Address _____

Endowment .... $ _____
Company _____
Policy # _____
Beneficiary _____
Address _____

Term .... $ _____
Company _____
Policy # _____
Beneficiary _____
Address _____

Term .... $ _____
Company _____
Policy # _____
Beneficiary _____
Address _____

Annuity Contract .... $ _____
Company _____
Contract # _____
Beneficiary _____
Address _____

Total Insurance .... $ _____

Accounts and notes receivable

(Debts payable to you may be left by will.)

Accounts .... $ _____
Due from _____
Address _____

Accounts .... $ _____
Due from _____
Address _____

Accounts .... $ _____
Due from _____
Address _____

Notes.. $ _____
Due from _____
Address _____

Notes.. $ _____
Due from _____
Address _____

Notes.. $ _____
Due from _____
Address _____

Other Debts... $ _____
Due from _____
Address _____

Other Debts... $ _____
Due from _____
Address _____

Other Debts... $ _____
Due from _____
Address _____

Total Accounts & Notes .... $ _____

Stocks and mutual funds

(Ownership of individually-held stock and mutual funds may be left by will.)

Company _____
CUSIP or Certificate # _____
and Type of shares _____
Value... $ _____

Company _____
CUSIP or Certificate # _____
and Type of shares _____
Value... $ _____

Company _____
CUSIP or Certificate # _____
and Type of shares _____
Value... $ _____

Company _____
CUSIP or Certificate # _____
and Type of shares _____
Value... $ _____

Company _____
CUSIP or Certificate # _____
and Type of shares _____
Value... $ _____

Company _____
CUSIP or Certificate # _____
and Type of shares _____
Value... $ _____

Company _____
CUSIP or Certificate # _____
and Type of shares _____
Value... $ _____

Total Stocks... $ _____

Bonds and mutual bond funds

(Ownership of individually-held bonds and mutual bond funds may be left by will.)

Company _____
CUSIP or Certificate # _____
and Type of shares _____
Value.. $ _____

Company _____
CUSIP or Certificate # _____
and Type of shares _____
Value.. $ _____

Company _____
CUSIP or Certificate # _____
and Type of shares _____
Value.. $ _____

Company _____
CUSIP or Certificate # _____
and Type of shares _____
Value.. $ _____

Company _____
CUSIP or Certificate # _____
and Type of shares _____
Value.. $ _____

Company _____
CUSIP or Certificate # _____
and Type of shares _____
Value.. $ _____

Company _____
CUSIP or Certificate # _____
and Type of shares _____
Value.. $ _____

Total Bonds .... $ _____

Business interests

(Ownership of business interests may generally be left by will.)

Individual Proprietorship
Name _____
Location _____
Type of business _____
Your net value.. $ _____

Individual Proprietorship
Name _____
Location _____
Type of business _____
Your net value.. $ _____

Interest in Partnership
Name _____
Location _____
Type of business _____
Gross value $_____
Percentage Interest _____
Your net value.. $ _____

Interest in Partnership
Name _____
Location _____
Type of business _____
Gross value $_____
Percentage Interest _____
Your net value.. $ _____

Close Corporation Interest
Name _____
Location _____
Type of business _____
Gross value $_____
Percentage shares held _____
Your net value.. $ _____

Total Business Value... $ _____

Real estate

(Property owned individually or as tenants-in-common may be left by will. Property held in joint tenancy or tenancy-by-entirety may not.)

<u>Personal residence</u>

Location _____
Value: $ _____
How held and percent held? (Joint Tenants, Tenancy in Common, etc?)
_____ / _____%
Value your share .... $ _____

<u>Vacation home</u>

Location _____
Value: $ _____
How held and percent held? (Joint Tenants, Tenancy in Common, etc?)
_____ / _____%
Value your share .... $ _____

<u>Vacant land</u>

Location _____
Value: $ _____
How held and percent held? (Joint Tenants, Tenancy in Common, etc?)
_____ / _____%
Value your share .... $ _____

<u>Income property</u>

Location _____
Value: $ _____
How held and percent held? (Joint Tenants, Tenancy in Common, etc?)
_____ / _____%
Value your share .... $ _____

Total Real Estate... $ _____

Personal property

(Personal property owned individually or as a tenant-in-common may be left by will.)

Car .... $ _____
Description _____

Car .... $ _____
Description _____

Boat/other vehicles .... $ _____
Description _____

Household furnishings .... $ _____
Description _____

Jewelry and furs .... $ _____
Description _____

Art work .... $ _____
Description _____

Total Personal Property .... $ _____

Miscellaneous assets

Royalties, Patents, Copyrights .... $ _____
Description _____

Heirlooms .... $ _____
Description _____

Other .... $ _____
Description _____

Other .... $ _____
Description _____

Total Miscellaneous .... $ _____

Employee benefit and pension/profit-sharing plans

(Retirement benefits can not be left by will.)

Company _____
Plan type _____
Net Value .... $ _____

Company _____
Plan type _____
Net Value .... $ _____

Company _____
Plan type _____
Net Value .... $ _____

Total Benefit Value	$ _____

Total Assets

(Insert totals from previous pages)

Cash Total.. $ _____
Life Insurance Total .... $ _____
Accounts & Notes Total .... $ _____
Stocks Total .... $ _____
Bonds Total.. $ _____
Business Total.. $ _____
Real Estate Total .... $ _____
Personal Property Total.. $ _____
Miscellaneous Total .... $ _____
Pension Total .... $ _____

TOTAL ASSETS...	$ _____

What are your liabilities?

Notes and loans payable

Payable to _____
Address _____
Term _____ Interest rate _____
Amount Due... $ _____

Payable to _____
Address _____
Term _____ Interest rate _____
Amount Due... $ _____

Total Notes and Loans Payable .... $ _____

Accounts payable

Payable to _____
Address _____
Term _____ Interest rate _____
Amount Due... $ _____

Payable to _____
Address _____
Term _____ Interest rate _____
Amount Due... $ _____

Total Accounts Payable .... $ _____

Mortgages payable

Property location _____

Payable to _____

Address _____

Term _____ Interest rate _____

Amount Due... $ _____

Property location _____

Payable to _____

Address _____

Term _____ Interest rate _____

Amount Due... $ _____

Total Mortgages Payable .... $ _____

Taxes due

Federal Income.. $ _____

State Income .... $ _____

Personal Property .... $ _____

Real Estate .... $ _____

Payroll .... $ _____

Other .... $ _____

Total Taxes Due .... $ _____

Credit card accounts

Credit Card Account #_____
Credit Card Company _____
Address _____
Amount Due... $ _____

Credit Card Account #_____
Credit Card Company _____
Address _____
Amount Due... $ _____

Total Credit Card Accounts Payable .... $ _____

Miscellaneous liabilities

To Whom Due _____
Address _____
Term _____ Interest rate _____
Amount Due... $ _____

To Whom Due _____
Address _____
Term _____ Interest rate _____
Amount Due... $ _____

Total Miscellaneous Liabilities .... $ _____

Total Liabilities

(Insert totals from previous pages)

Total Notes and Loans Payable .... $ _____
Total Accounts Payable .... $ _____
Total Mortgages Payable .... $ _____
Total Taxes Due .... $ _____
Total Credit Card Accounts .... $ _____
Total Miscellaneous Liabilities .... $ _____

TOTAL LIABILITIES.. $ _____

Net Worth Of Your Estate

Total Assets... $ _____

minus (-)

Total Liabilities... $ _____

equals (=)

YOUR TOTAL NET WORTH... $ _____

Chapter 4

Beneficiary Questionnaire

In this chapter you will determine both who you would like your beneficiaries to be and what specific property you will leave each in your will. First, there is a brief discussion regarding who may be a beneficiary. Next, there is an explanation of the various methods that you may use to leave gifts to your beneficiaries. Finally, there is a Beneficiary Questionnaire which you will use to actually make the decisions regarding which beneficiaries will receive which property.

Who may be a beneficiary?

Any person or organization who receives property under a will is termed a *beneficiary* of that will. Much the same as there are certain requirements that the person signing the will must meet, there are certain requirements relating to who may receive property under a will. These generally, however, are in the form of negative requirements. Stated in another way, this means that any person or organization may receive property under a will unless they fall into certain narrow categories of disqualification.

Besides these few exceptions noted below, any person or organization you choose may receive property under your will. This includes any family members, the named executor, any illegitimate children (if named specifically), corporations, charities (but see below on possible restrictions), creditors, debtors, and any friends, acquaintances, or even strangers.

The few categories of disqualified beneficiaries are as follows:

☒ An attorney who drafts the will is generally assumed to have used undue influence if he or she is made a beneficiary.

☒ Many states disqualify any witnesses to the execution of the will. Check the Appendix to see if your state has this restriction. However, to be safe, it is recommended that none of your witnesses be beneficiaries under your will.

☒ A person who murders a testator is universally disqualified from receiving any property under the murdered person's will.

☒ An unincorporated association is typically not allowed to receive property under a will. This particular disqualification stems from the fact that such associations generally have no legal right to hold property.

A few states also have restrictions on the right to leave property to charitable organizations and churches. These restrictions are usually in two forms: a time limit prior to death when changes to a will which leave large amounts of money or property to a charitable organization are disallowed and also a percentage limit on the amount of a person's estate which may be left to a charitable organization (often a limit of 50%). The reasoning behind this rule is to prevent abuse of a dying person's desire to be forgiven. There have been, in the past, unscrupulous individuals or organizations who have obtained last minute changes in a will in an attempt to have the bulk of a person's estate left to them or their group. If you intend to leave large sums of money or property to a charitable organization or church, please check the Appendix to see if there are any restrictions of this type in force in your state.

Under this same category as to who may be a beneficiary under your will are several points related to marriage, divorce, and children. First and foremost, you are advised to review your will periodically and make any necessary changes as your marital or family situation may dictate. If you are divorced, married, remarried, or widowed, adopt or have a child, there may be unforeseen consequences based on the way you have written your will. Each state has differing laws on the effect of marriage and divorce on a person's will. In some states, divorce entirely revokes a will as to the divorced spouse. In others, divorce has no effect and your divorced spouse may inherit your estate if you do not change your will. Marriage and the birth of children are also treated somewhat differently by each state. You are advised to review the Appendix as it relates to these aspects of your life and prepare your will accordingly.

Your will should be prepared with regard to how your life is presently arranged. It should, however, always be reviewed and updated each time there is a substantial change in your life.

What types of gifts may you make?

There are various standard terms and phrases that may be employed when making gifts under your will. The will clauses which are employed in this book incorporate these standard terms. Using these standard phrases, you may make a gift of any property that you will own at your death to any beneficiary whom you choose (remembering the few disqualified types of beneficiaries).

A few type of gifts are possible but are not addressed in the wills that may be prepared using this book. Simple shared gifts (for example: I give all my property to my children, Alice, Bill, and Carl, in equal shares) are possible using this book. However, any complex shared gift arrangements will require the assistance of an attorney. In addition, you may impose simple conditions on any gifts in wills prepared using this book. However, complex conditional gifts which impose detailed requirements that the beneficiary must comply with in order to receive the gift are also beyond the scope of this book. Finally, although it is possible to leave any gifts under your will in many types of trusts, a simple trust for leaving gifts to children is the only trust available for wills prepared using this book. If you desire to leave property in trust to an adult or in a complex trust arrangement, you are advised to seek professional advice.

The terms that you use to make any gifts can be any that you desire, as long as the gift is made in a clear and understandable manner. Someone reading the will at a later date, perhaps even a stranger appointed by a court, must be able to determine exactly what property you intended to be a gift and exactly who it is you intended to receive it. If you follow the few rules which follow regarding how to identify your gifts and beneficiaries, your intentions will be clear to whomever may need to interpret your will in the future:

1. Always describe the property in as detailed and clear a manner as possible. For example: do not simply state "my car"; instead state "my 1994 Buick Skylark, Serial #123456789". Describe exactly what it is you wish for each beneficiary to receive. You may make any type of gift that you wish, either a cash gift, a gift of a specific piece of personal property or real estate, or a specific share of your total estate. If you wish to give some of your estate in the form of portions of the total, it is recommended to use fractional portions. For example, if you wish to leave your estate in equal shares to two persons, use "I give one-half of my total estate to . . . " for each party.

In your description of the property, you should be as specific and precise as possible. For land, it is suggested that you use the description exactly as shown on the deed to the property. For personal property, be certain that your description clearly differentiates your gift from any other property.

2. Always describe the beneficiaries is as precise and clear a manner as is possible. For example: do not simply state "my son"; instead state "my son, Robert Edward Smith, of Houston Texas". This is particularly important if the beneficiary is an adopted child.

3. Never provide a gift to a group or class of people without specifically stating their individual names. For example: do not simply state "my sisters"; instead state "my sister Katherine Mary Jones, and my sister Elizabeth Anne Jones, and my sister Annette Josephine Jones".

4. You may put simple conditions on the gift if they are reasonable and not immoral or illegal. For example: you may say "This gift is to be used to purchase day care equipment for the church nursery"; but you may not say "I give this gift to my sister only if she divorces her deadbeat husband Ralph Edwards".

5. You should always provide for an alternate beneficiary for the purpose of allowing you to designate someone to receive the gift if your first choice to receive the gift dies before you do (or, in the case of a organization chosen as primary beneficiary, is no longer in business). Your choice for alternate beneficiary may be one or more persons or an organization. In addition, you may delete the alternate beneficiary choice and substitute the words "the residue" instead. The result of this change will be that if your primary beneficiary dies before you do, your gift will pass under your residuary clause, which is discussed next.

6. Although not a technical legal requirement, it is strongly recommended that a residuary clause be included in every will. With it, you will choose the person, persons, or organization to receive anything not covered by other clauses of your will. Even if you feel that you have given away everything that you own under other clauses of your will, this can be a very important clause.

If, for any reason, any other gifts under your will are not able to completed, this clause takes effect. For example, if a beneficiary refuses to accept your gift or the chosen beneficiary has died and no alternate was selected or both the beneficiary and alternate has died, the gift will be returned to your estate and would pass under the "residuary clause". If there is no "residuary clause" included in your will, any property not disposed of under your will is treated as though you did not have a will and could potentially be forfeited to the state. To avoid this, it is strongly recommended that you make this clause mandatory in your will.

7.   A survivorship clause should be included in every will. This provides for a period of survival for any beneficiary. For wills prepared using this book, the period is set at 30 days. The practical effect of this is to be certain that your property passes under your will and not that of a beneficiary who dies shortly after receiving your gift.

Without this clause in your will it would be possible that property would momentarily pass to a beneficiary under your will. When that person dies (possibly immediately if a result of a common accident or disaster) your property could wind up being left to the person whom your beneficiary designated, rather than to your alternate beneficiary.

8.   To disinherit anyone from receiving property under your will you should specifically name the person to be disinherited, rather than simply rely upon simply not mentioning them in your will. To disinherit children and grandchildren of deceased children, they must be mentioned specifically. In the case of children born after a will is executed and of spouses of a marriage which takes place after a will is executed, there are differing provisions in many states as to the effect of their not being mentioned in a will. Please see the Appendix for information regarding the laws in your particular state. The safest method, however, is to specifically mention anyone to be disinherited. Be sure to clearly identify the person being disinherited by full name. Another legal method to achieve approximately the same result as disinheritance is to leave the person a very small amount (at least $1.00) as a gift in your will. Also, be sure to review your will each time there is a change in your family circumstances. Please see Chapter 11 for a discussion regarding changing your will.

9.   Finally, property may be left to your children in trust using the Children's Trust Clause that is included in Chapters 6 and 7. Please refer to the discussion of that clause in those chapters.

If you state your gifts simply, clearly, and accurately, you can be assured that they will be able to be carried out after your death regardless of who may be required to interpret the language in your will.

Beneficiary Questionnaire
Who will receive which of your assets?

Spouse _____

    Maiden Name _____

    Date of Marriage _____

    Date of Birth _____

    Address _____

    _____

    Current Income $ _____

    Amount, specific items, or share of estate which you desire to leave _____

    _____

    _____

    Alternate Beneficiary _____

Child _____

    Date of Birth _____

    Address _____

    _____

    Spouse's Name (if any) _____

    Current Income $ _____

    Amount, specific items, or share of estate which you desire to leave _____

    _____

    _____

    Alternate Beneficiary _____

Child _____

    Date of Birth _____

    Address _____

    _____

    Spouse's Name (if any) _____

    Current Income $ _____

    Amount, specific items, or share of estate which you desire to leave _____

    _____

    _____

    Alternate Beneficiary _____

Children

Child _____
    Date of Birth _____
    Address _____
    _____
    Spouse's Name (if any) _____
    Current Income $ _____
    Amount, specific items, or share of estate which you desire to leave _____
    _____
    _____
    Alternate Beneficiary _____

Child _____
    Date of Birth _____
    Address _____
    _____
    Spouse's Name (if any) _____
    Current Income $ _____
    Amount, specific items, or share of estate which you desire to leave _____
    _____
    _____
    Alternate Beneficiary _____

Child _____
    Date of Birth _____
    Address _____
    _____
    Spouse's Name (if any) _____
    Current Income $ _____
    Amount, specific items, or share of estate which you desire to leave _____
    _____
    _____
    Alternate Beneficiary _____

Grandchildren

Grandchild _____
    Date of Birth _____
    Address _____
    _____
    Spouse's Name (if any) _____
    Current Income $ _____
    Amount, specific items, or share of estate which you desire to leave _____
    _____
    _____
    Alternate Beneficiary _____

Grandchild _____
    Date of Birth _____
    Address _____
    _____
    Spouse's Name (if any) _____
    Current Income $ _____
    Amount, specific items, or share of estate which you desire to leave _____
    _____
    _____
    Alternate Beneficiary _____

Grandchild _____
    Date of Birth _____
    Address _____
    _____
    Spouse's Name (if any) _____
    Current Income $ _____
    Amount, specific items, or share of estate which you desire to leave _____
    _____
    _____
    Alternate Beneficiary _____

Grandchildren

Grandchild _____
    Date of Birth _____
    Address _____

    _____
    Spouse's Name (if any) _____
    Current Income $ _____
    Amount, specific items, or share of estate which you desire to leave _____

    _____

    _____
    Alternate Beneficiary _____

Grandchild _____
    Date of Birth _____
    Address _____

    _____
    Spouse's Name (if any) _____
    Current Income $ _____
    Amount, specific items, or share of estate which you desire to leave _____

    _____

    _____
    Alternate Beneficiary _____

Grandchild _____
    Date of Birth _____
    Address _____

    _____
    Spouse's Name (if any) _____
    Current Income $ _____
    Amount, specific items, or share of estate which you desire to leave _____

    _____

    _____
    Alternate Beneficiary _____

Parents and siblings

Parent _____

    Date of Birth _____

    Address _____

    _____

    Spouse's Name (if any) _____

    Current Income $ _____

    Amount, specific items, or share of estate which you desire to leave _____

    _____

    _____

    Alternate Beneficiary _____

Parent _____

    Date of Birth _____

    Address _____

    _____

    Spouse's Name (if any) _____

    Current Income $ _____

    Amount, specific items, or share of estate which you desire to leave _____

    _____

    _____

    Alternate Beneficiary _____

Sibling _____

    Date of Birth _____

    Address _____

    _____

    Spouse's Name (if any) _____

    Current Income $ _____

    Amount, specific items, or share of estate which you desire to leave _____

    _____

    _____

    Alternate Beneficiary _____

Siblings

Sibling _____

    Date of Birth _____

    Address _____

    _____

    Spouse's Name (if any) _____

    Current Income $ _____

    Amount, specific items, or share of estate which you desire to leave _____

    _____

    _____

    Alternate Beneficiary _____

Sibling _____

    Date of Birth _____

    Address _____

    _____

    Spouse's Name (if any) _____

    Current Income $ _____

    Amount, specific items, or share of estate which you desire to leave _____

    _____

    _____

    Alternate Beneficiary _____

Sibling _____

    Date of Birth _____

    Address _____

    _____

    Spouse's Name (if any) _____

    Current Income $ _____

    Amount, specific items, or share of estate which you desire to leave _____

    _____

    _____

    Alternate Beneficiary _____

Other dependents

Other Dependent _____
    Date of Birth _____
    Address _____
    _____
    Spouse's Name (if any) _____
    Current Income $ _____
    Amount, specific items, or share of estate which you desire to leave _____
    _____
    _____
    Alternate Beneficiary _____

Other Dependent _____
    Date of Birth _____
    Address _____
    _____
    Spouse's Name (if any) _____
    Current Income $ _____
    Amount, specific items, or share of estate which you desire to leave _____
    _____
    _____
    Alternate Beneficiary _____

Other Dependent _____
    Date of Birth _____
    Address _____
    _____
    Spouse's Name (if any) _____
    Current Income $ _____
    Amount, specific items, or share of estate which you desire to leave _____
    _____
    _____
    Alternate Beneficiary _____

Other relatives, friends, or organizations that you wish to leave gifts?

Name _____

    Relationship _____

    Address _____

    _____

    Spouse's Name (if any) _____

    Current Income $ _____

    Amount, specific items, or share of estate which you desire to leave _____

    _____

    _____

    Alternate Beneficiary _____

Name _____

    Relationship _____

    Address _____

    _____

    Spouse's Name (if any) _____

    Current Income $ _____

    Amount, specific items, or share of estate which you desire to leave _____

    _____

    _____

    Alternate Beneficiary _____

Name _____

    Relationship _____

    Address _____

    _____

    Spouse's Name (if any) _____

    Current Income $ _____

    Amount, specific items, or share of estate which you desire to leave _____

    _____

    _____

    Alternate Beneficiary _____

Other relatives, friends, or organizations

Name _____
    Relationship _____
    Address _____
    _____
    Spouse's Name (if any) _____
    Current Income $ _____
    Amount, specific items, or share of estate which you desire to leave _____
    _____
    _____
    Alternate Beneficiary _____

Name _____
    Relationship _____
    Address _____
    _____
    Spouse's Name (if any) _____
    Current Income $ _____
    Amount, specific items, or share of estate which you desire to leave _____
    _____
    _____
    Alternate Beneficiary _____

Name _____
    Relationship _____
    Address _____
    _____
    Spouse's Name (if any) _____
    Current Income $ _____
    Amount, specific items, or share of estate which you desire to leave _____
    _____
    _____
    Alternate Beneficiary _____

Any persons whom you wish to specifically leave out of your will?

Name _____
    Relationship _____
    Address _____
    _____
    Spouse's Name (if any) _____
    Current Income $ _____
    Reason for disinheritance: _____
    _____

Name _____
    Relationship _____
    Address _____
    _____
    Spouse's Name (if any) _____
    Current Income $ _____
    Reason for disinheritance: _____
    _____

Name _____
    Relationship _____
    Address _____
    _____
    Spouse's Name (if any) _____
    Current Income $ _____
    Reason for disinheritance: _____
    _____

Chapter 5

Information For Executor

In this chapter, various information relating to the executor of your will and the probate process is provided. Before actually planning your will, an overview of how the legal system operates after a person's death may be useful to keep in mind. The system of court administration of the estates of deceased parties is generally entitled *probate*. How to avoid the probate court was the subject of one of the first self-help law books to challenge the legal establishment's monopoly on law. Probate, however, despite what many lawyers would have you believe, is not all that mysterious a matter.

Overview of a Typical Probate Proceeding

Upon a person's death in most states, there is a general sequence of events which takes place. First, the executor appointed in the will (who, hopefully, has been notified of her or his duties in advance) locates the will and files it with the proper authority. If necessary, the executor arranges for the funeral and burial. If it is a complicated or very large estate, it may be prudent to hire a lawyer to handle the probate proceeding. Upon presenting the will to the probate court, the will is *proved*, which means that it is determined whether or not the document presented is actually the deceased's will. This may be done in most states with a "Self-Proving Affidavit" which is prepared and notarized at the time your will is signed (See Chapter 6).

Upon proof that it is a valid will, the executor is officially given legal authority to gather together all of the estate's property. This authority for the executor to administer the estate is generally referred to as *letters testamentary*. The probate court also officially appoints the parties who are designated as guardians of any minor children and any trustees.

If no executor was chosen in the will, or if the one chosen can not serve, the probate court will appoint one. The order of preference for appointment is commonly as follows: surviving spouse, next of kin, a person having an interest in the estate or claims against the estate.

If the will is shown to be invalid, or if there is no will, the same sequence of events generally is followed. However, in this case, the party appointed to administer the estate is usually titled an *administrator* of the estate rather than an executor. The court orders granting authority to an administrator are generally referred to as *letters of administration*.

After the executor or administrator is given authority, he or she handles the collection of assets, the management of the estate, and the payment of any debts and taxes until such time as all creditor's claims have been satisfied and other business of the estate completed. An inventory of all of the assets is typically the first official act of an executor. Creditors, by the way, only have a certain time period in which to make a claim against an estate. The same holds true for any *contests* of the will (challenging the validity of a will). Contesting a will is a fairly rare occurrence and is most difficult if the will was properly prepared and signed by a competent, sane adult.

The executor will generally also be empowered under state law to provide an allowance for the surviving spouse and children until such time as all affairs of the deceased person are completed and the estate is closed.

Upon completion of all business and payment of all outstanding charges against the estate, an accounting and inventory of the estate's assets are then presented to the probate court by the executor. At this time, if everything appears to be in order, the executor is generally empowered to distribute all of the remaining property to the persons or organizations named in the will and probate is officially closed. The entire probate process generally takes from 4 to 18 months to complete. The distribution of your property and money is usually handled solely by the executor (possibly with a lawyer's help to be certain that all legal requirements are fulfilled). Normally, this is done without further court approval of the disbursement.

Choosing an Executor

Your choice of who should be your executor is a personal decision. A spouse, sibling, or other trusted party is usually chosen to act as executor, although a bank officer, accountant, or attorney may also be chosen. The person chosen should be someone you trust and someone that you feel can handle or at least efficiently delegate the complicated tasks of making an inventory of all of your property and distributing it to your chosen beneficiaries. The person chosen should be a resident of the state in which you currently reside. In addition, all states require that executors be competent, of legal age (generally, over 18) and a citizen of the U.S. Although it is possible, it is generally not wise to appoint two or more persons as co-executors. It is preferable to appoint your first choice as primary executor and the other person as alternate executor.

In your will, you will grant the executor broad powers to manage your estate and also provide that he or she not be required to post a bond in order to be appointed to serve as executor. This provision can save your estate considerable money, depending upon its size. The fees for executor bonds are based upon the size of the estate and can amount to hundreds of dollars every year that your estate is being managed. By waiving this bond requirement, these potential bond fees can be eliminated and the money saved passed on to your beneficiaries.

You should discuss your choice with the person chosen to be certain that they will be willing to act as executor. In addition, it is wise to provide your executor, in advance, with a copy of the will, a copy of any organ-donation desires, a copy of your Property and Beneficiary Questionnaires, and a copy of the information contained in this chapter.

Executor Checklist

Provided here is a checklist of items that your executor may have to deal with after your death. Although this list is extensive, there may be other personal tasks that are not included. Scanning this list can give you an idea of the scope and range of the executor's duties. You can provide invaluable assistance to your executor by being aware of their duties and providing them with information to help them. This listing is divided into various time periods (Immediate, 1st week, 1st month, long-term). These time period are approximations and many of the duties may be required to be performed either before or after the exact time specified. Following this list, a section is provided for listing such information for your executor.

Immediate Executor Duties

- ☐ Contact mortuary or funeral home regarding services.
- ☐ Contact cemetery regarding burial or cremation.
- ☐ Contact local newspaper with obituary information.
- ☐ Contact relatives and close friends.
- ☐ Contact employer and business associates.
- ☐ Contact lawyer and accountant.
- ☐ Arrange for pall bearers.
- ☐ Contact guardians or trustees named in will.
- ☐ Arrange for immediate care of decedent's children.
- ☐ Arrange for living expenses for decedent's spouse.
- ☐ Contact veterans organizations.

Executor Duties Within 1st Week

- ☐ Contact life insurance agent and report death.
- ☐ Contact general insurance agent.
- ☐ Contact medical and health insurance companies.
- ☐ Contact Medicare.
- ☐ Contact union regarding pensions and death benefits.
- ☐ Contact employer regarding pensions and death benefits.
- ☐ Contact military regarding pensions and death benefits.
- ☐ Contact Social Security Administration.
- ☐ Obtain death certificates from attending physician.
- ☐ Contact banks, savings and loans, and credit unions.
- ☐ Contact mortgage companies.
- ☐ Contact IRA or KEOGH account trustees.
- ☐ Contact stock broker and investment counselor.
- ☐ Contact county recorder.
- ☐ Contact post office.
- ☐ Contact Department of Motor Vehicles.
- ☐ Arrange for management of business or real estate holdings.
- ☐ Review all of decedent's records and legal documents.

Executor Duties Within 1st Month

- ☐ Contact gas, telephone, electric, trash, and water companies.
- ☐ Contact newspaper and magazine subscription departments.
- ☐ Contact credit card companies.

❑　Begin inventory of assets.
❑　Arrange for appraisal of assets.
❑　Begin collection of assets.
❑　Open bank accounts for estate.
❑　Open decedent's safe deposit box.

Long Term Executor Duties

❑　File the will with probate court.
❑　Inventory all estate assets.
❑　Collect all monies and property due to decedent.
❑　Pay all taxes due and file tax returns.
❑　Provide notice to all creditors of time limit for claims.
❑　Pay all debts and expenses of decedent, including funeral expenses..
❑　Arrange for sale of estate assets, if necessary.
❑　Distribute all remaining assets according to will.
❑　Submit final accounting and receipts to probate court.
❑　Close estate books and affairs.

Executor Information List

The following listing will provide your executor with valuable information that will make performance of their difficult task much easier. Included in this questionnaire is information relating to the location of your records, any funeral or burial arrangements that you have made, lists of important persons which the executor will need to contact after your death, and information that will assist your executor in preparing any obituary listing. It may be very difficult to confront the need for this information. Please take the time to provide this valuable record of information for your executor. After your death, they may be under tremendous emotional stress and this information will help them perform their necessary duties with the least difficulty. You will probably wish to give this information list and a copy of your will to the person whom you have chosen as your executor.

Executor Information List

Location of Records

Original of will:
Original of codicil:
Trust documents:
Safe deposit box and key:
Bank book and savings passbook:
Treasury bills and certificates of deposit:
Social Security records:
Real estate deeds and mortgage documents:
Veteran's information:
Stock certificates and bonds:
Promissory notes and loan documents:
Business records:
Partnership records:
Corporation records:
Automobile titles:
Income tax records:
Credit card records:
Birth certificate:
Warranties:

Funeral or Cremation Arrangements

Name of mortuary, funeral service, or crematorium: _____
    Name of person contacted: _____
    Phone #: _____
    Address: _____
    _____
    _____
    Arrangements made: _____
    _____
    _____
    _____
    _____

Name of cemetery: _____
    Name of person contacted: _____
    Phone #: _____
    Address: _____
    _____
    _____
    Arrangements made: _____
    _____
    _____
    _____
    _____

Location of memorial or church service: _____
    Name of person contacted: _____
    Phone #: _____
    Address: _____
    _____
    _____
    Arrangements made: _____
    _____
    _____
    _____
    _____

Persons to Contact

Clergy: _____
    Address: _____
    City, State, Zip: _____
    Phone: _____

Lawyer: _____
    Address: _____
    City, State, Zip: _____
    Phone: _____

Accountant: _____
    Address: _____
    City, State, Zip: _____
    Phone: _____

Life Insurance Agent: _____
    Address: _____
    City, State, Zip: _____
    Phone: _____

General Insurance Agent: _____
    Address: _____
    City, State, Zip: _____
    Phone: _____

Employer: _____
    Address: _____
    City, State, Zip: _____
    Phone: _____

Military Unit: _____
    Address: _____
    City, State, Zip: _____
    Phone: _____

Persons to Contact

Relative name: _____
    Address: _____
    City, State, Zip: _____
    Phone: _____

Relative name: _____
    Address: _____
    City, State, Zip: _____
    Phone: _____

Relative name: _____
    Address: _____
    City, State, Zip: _____
    Phone: _____

Relative name: _____
    Address: _____
    City, State, Zip: _____
    Phone: _____

Relative name: _____
    Address: _____
    City, State, Zip: _____
    Phone: _____

Relative name: _____
    Address: _____
    City, State, Zip: _____
    Phone: _____

Relative name: _____
    Address: _____
    City, State, Zip: _____
    Phone: _____

Persons to Contact

Friend name: _____
    Address: _____
    City, State, Zip: _____
    Phone: _____

Friend name: _____
    Address: _____
    City, State, Zip: _____
    Phone: _____

Friend name: _____
    Address: _____
    City, State, Zip: _____
    Phone: _____

Friend name: _____
    Address: _____
    City, State, Zip: _____
    Phone: _____

Friend name: _____
    Address: _____
    City, State, Zip: _____
    Phone: _____

Friend name: _____
    Address: _____
    City, State, Zip: _____
    Phone: _____

Friend name: _____
    Address: _____
    City, State, Zip: _____
    Phone: _____

Newspaper Obituary Information:

Name:	
Date of birth:	
Place of birth:	
Current residence:	
Former residence:	
Occupation:	
Education:	
Military service:	
Club, union, civic, or fraternal organizations:	
Special achievements:	
Survivors:	
Date of death:	
Place of service:	
Date of service:	
Time of service:	
Memorial contribution preference:	

Chapter 6

Will Clauses

This chapter contains a listing of all of the necessary will clauses which you will need to complete your own will. Although not every possible contingency is covered by these clauses, most choices for dispositions under your will should be covered by the clauses shown in this chapter. By following the instruction in this chapter, you will be shown how to custom-tailor a will to exactly fit your own individual circumstances. These same will clauses have been assembled into basic wills for use in certain specific personal situations in Chapter 7. Please read that chapter to determine if one of the pre-assembled wills would be appropriate in your circumstances.

Using the clauses in this Chapter you will be able to prepare a will in which you may:

❑   Make specific gifts of cash, real estate, or personal property to anyone;
❑   Make specific gifts of to anyone;
❑   Make specific gifts of certain shares of your estate;
❑   Disinherit anyone from receiving anything from your estate;
❑   Make a gift of the rest (*residue*) of your assets to anyone;
❑   Choose an executor to administer your estate;
❑   Choose a guardian for any minor children;
❑   Set up a trust and choose a trustee for children's gifts;
❑   Declare your intention to be an organ donor;
❑   Declare your choice for funeral/cremation arrangements.

Instructions

To prepare your will using the clauses in this chapter, please follow these step-by-step instructions:

1.   Carefully read through this entire chapter. Then, select those clauses you desire to use in your will and make a photo-copy of each clause you have chosen. These photo-copies will serve as your worksheets. You may, if you wish, simply use this book as a worksheet and fill-in the information directly onto the pages of this book (unless you are borrowing this book from a library!) Please note that there are certain clauses which are mandatory for all wills and you must include these clauses in your own will. These mandatory clauses are clearly marked for your ease in preparing your will.

2.   In choosing your own individual clauses, simply follow the directions and instructions which are given immediately prior to each specific clause and fill in the appropriate blanks as indicated. As you are choosing and preparing your specific will clauses, it is suggested that you have before you the completed Property and Beneficiary Questionnaires from Chapters 3 and 4. The information which you compiled for those Questionnaires will be your guide for preparing your will, both in terms of being certain that you have disposed of all of your assets and in terms of being certain that you have left gifts to all those persons or organizations that you wished to.

3.   When you have completed your selection of clauses and filled in all of the appropriate information, read through them carefully to be sure that you have filled in the blanks exactly to your wishes. Then starting at the beginning of your will clauses, cross out all of the words and phrases that do not apply in your situation. All of the identification lines under the blanks should also be crossed out as you will not be typing them on your final will.

4.   Finally, when you are satisfied that you have filled in the information on your worksheet will correctly, read through the sample will contained in Chapter 8 to see how a completed will is arranged. Following that, turn to Chapter 9 for instructions on typing and preparing your will for signature.

Will Clauses

Title

Mandatory: The below title is mandatory for all wills and must be included. Fill in the name blank with your full legal name. If you have been known under more than one name, use your principal name. Do not number this title.

Last Will and Testament of _____
[your full name]

Identification Clause

Mandatory. This clause must be included in all wills. Do not number this clause. In the first blank, include any other names which you are known by. Do this by adding the phrase: "also known as" after your principal full name. For example: *John James Smith, also known as Jimmy John Smith.* In the spaces provided for your residence, use the location of your principal residence (where you currently live permanently).

I, _____, a resident
[your full name and any other names that you have used]
of _____, _____,
[name of city or town]   [name of county]
_____, declare that this is my
[name of state]
Last Will and Testament and I revoke all previous wills and codicils.

Marital Status Clause (Unmarried and no children)

Mandatory if you are unmarried and have no children. If used, number this clause #1 in the box.

☐ I have never been married and I have no children.

Marital Status Clause (Currently married)

Mandatory if you are currently married. If used, number this clause #1 in the box.

☐ I am married to _____.
[spouse's full name]

Marital Status Clause (Previously married)

Mandatory if you have been previously married. If you use this clause, number it consecutively.

☐ I was previously married to _____.
[previous spouse's full name]
That marriage ended on _____, 19 _____,
[date]
by _____.
[death, divorce, or annulment]

Children Identification Clause

Mandatory if you have any children who are living. If you need more spaces than are shown, simply repeat the information. Number this clause consecutively.

☐ I have _____ children living. Their names, addresses, and
       [number of children]
dates of birth are as follows:

_____
[Child's name]
_____
[Child's address]
_____

_____
[Child's date of birth]

_____
[Child's name]
_____
[Child's address]
_____

_____
[Child's date of birth]

_____
[Child's name]
_____
[Child's address]
_____

_____
[Child's date of birth]

_____
[Child's name]

_____
[Child's address]

_____

_____
[Child's date of birth]

_____
[Child's name]

_____
[Child's address]

_____

_____
[Child's date of birth]

_____
[Child's name]

_____
[Child's address]

_____

_____
[Child's date of birth]

_____
[Child's name]

_____
[Child's address]

_____

_____
[Child's date of birth]

Grandchildren Identification Clause

Mandatory if you have any grandchildren living. Insert each grandchild's name, address, and date of birth. Number this clause consecutively.

☐ I have _____ grandchildren living. Their names,
       [number of Grandchildren]
addresses, and dates of birth are as follows:

_____
       [Grandchild's name]
_____
       [Grandchild's address]
_____

_____
       [Grandchild's date of birth]

_____
       [Grandchild's name]
_____
       [Grandchild's address]
_____

_____
       [Grandchild's date of birth]

_____
       [Grandchild's name]
_____
       [Grandchild's address]
_____

_____
       [Grandchild's date of birth]

_____
[Grandchild's name]

_____
[Grandchild's address]

_____

_____
[Grandchild's date of birth]

_____
[Grandchild's name]

_____
[Grandchild's address]

_____

_____
[Grandchild's date of birth]

_____
[Grandchild's name]

_____
[Grandchild's address]

_____

_____
[Grandchild's date of birth]

_____
[Grandchild's name]

_____
[Grandchild's address]

_____

_____
[Grandchild's date of birth]

Entire Estate Gift Clause

Optional: Use this clause if you are leaving all of your property to one person or organization. Many people choose to leave their entire estate to their spouse or some other individual. Where you are asked in the clause to state the beneficiary's relationship, simply state their kinship, (for example: *my wife*), their status as a friend or co-worker, or the status as an organization (for example: *my church* or *my alma mater*). If you use this clause, do not use any other clause which leaves a gift to another person or organization. However, you should still use the residuary clause which is explained later. If you desire to leave portions of your estate to more than one person or organization, do not use this particular clause. Rather, use one or more of the "Specific Gift" clauses that follow.

You should always name an alternate beneficiary. The choice of alternate beneficiary is for the purpose of allowing you to designate someone to receive the gift if your first choice to receive the gift dies before you do (or, in the case of a organization chosen as primary beneficiary, is no longer in business), or refuses the gift. In this or any of the other gift clauses, your choice for alternate beneficiary may be one or more persons or an organization. It is recommended to always specifically name your beneficiary(s), rather than using a description only, such as "my children". In addition, you may delete the alternate beneficiary choice and substitute the words "the residue" instead. The result of this change will be that if your primary beneficiary dies before you do, your gift to pass under your residuary clause, which is discussed later in this chapter.

Be sure to clearly identify the beneficiary and alternate beneficiary by full name. You can also name joint beneficiaries, such as several children, if you choose. The space provided for an identification of the relationship of the beneficiary can be simply a descriptive phrase like "my wife", or "my brother-in-law", or "my best friend". It does not mean that the beneficiary must be related to you personally. If used, number this clause consecutively.

☐ I give my entire estate to _____,
　　　　　　　　　　　　　　　　[name of beneficiary]

my _____, or if not surviving
　　[relationship of beneficiary]

to _____,
　　[name of alternate beneficiary]

my _____.
　　[relationship of alternate beneficiary]

Specific Gifts Clause

Optional: Use the following line and the paragraphs that follow as one entire clause. Number the whole clause consecutively. Use as many of the "I give . . ." paragraphs as is necessary to complete your chosen gifts. In these paragraphs, you may make any type of gift that you wish, either a cash gift, a gift of a specific piece of personal property or real estate, or a specific share of your total estate. If you wish to give some of your estate in the form of portions of the total, it is recommended to use fractional portions. For example, if you wish to leave your estate in equal shares to two persons, use "I give one-half of my total estate to . . . " for each party.

In your description of the property, you should be as specific and precise as possible. For land, it is suggested that you use the description exactly as shown on the deed to the property. For personal property, be certain that your description clearly differentiates your gift from any other property. For example: "I give my blue velvet coat which was a gift from my brother John to . . . ". Use serial numbers, colors, or any other descriptive words to clearly indicate the exact nature of the gift. For cash gifts, specifically indicate the amount of the gift. For gifts of securities, state the amount of shares and the name of the company. You may add simple conditions to the gifts that you make, if you desire. For example: You may state "I give $1,000 to the Centerville Church for use in purchasing a new roof for the church". Complex conditions, however, are not possible in this clause, and immoral or illegal conditions are not acceptable.

Be sure to clearly identify the beneficiary and alternate beneficiary by full name. You can also name joint beneficiaries, such as several children, if you choose. The space provided for an identification of the relationship of the beneficiary can be simply a descriptive phrase like "my wife", or "my brother-in-law", or "my best friend". It does not mean that the beneficiary must be related to you personally.

The choice of alternate beneficiary is for the purpose of allowing you to designate someone to receive the gift if your first choice to receive the gift dies before you do (or, in the case of a organization chosen as primary beneficiary, is no longer in business). In this or any of the other gift clauses, your choice for alternate beneficiary may be one or more persons or an organization. It is recommended to always specifically name your beneficiary(s), rather than using a description only, such as "my children". In addition, you may delete the alternate beneficiary choice and substitute the words "the residue" instead. The result of this change will be that if your primary beneficiary dies before you do, your gift to pass under your residuary clause, which is discussed later in this chapter.

Space is provided for 6 individual specific gifts. If additional gifts are desired, simply photo-copy an additional page. If used, number this clause consecutively.

☐ I make the following specific gifts:

I give _____

_____
       [complete description of property]
to _____,
     [name of beneficiary]
my _____, or if not surviving
     [relationship of beneficiary]
to_____,
     [name of alternate beneficiary]
my _____.
     [relationship of alternate beneficiary]

I give _____

_____
       [complete description of property]
to _____,
     [name of beneficiary]
my _____, or if not surviving
     [relationship of beneficiary]
to_____,
     [name of alternate beneficiary]
my _____.
     [relationship of alternate beneficiary]

I give _____

_____
       [complete description of property]
to _____,
     [name of beneficiary]
my _____, or if not surviving
     [relationship of beneficiary]
to_____,
     [name of alternate beneficiary]
my _____.
     [relationship of alternate beneficiary]

I give _____

_____
         [complete description of property]
to _____,
      [name of beneficiary]
my _____, or if not surviving
      [relationship of beneficiary]
to_____,
      [name of alternate beneficiary]
my _____.
      [relationship of alternate beneficiary]

I give _____

_____
         [complete description of property]
to _____,
      [name of beneficiary]
my _____, or if not surviving
      [relationship of beneficiary]
to_____,
      [name of alternate beneficiary]
my _____.
      [relationship of alternate beneficiary]

I give _____

_____
         [complete description of property]
to _____,
      [name of beneficiary]
my _____, or if not surviving
      [relationship of beneficiary]
to_____,
      [name of alternate beneficiary]
my _____.
      [relationship of alternate beneficiary]

Residuary Clause

Mandatory: Although not a technical legal requirement, it is strongly recommended that this clause be included in every will. It should be numbered consecutively. With it, you will choose the person, persons, or organization to receive anything not covered by other clauses of your will. Even if you feel that you have given away everything that you own under other clauses of your will, this can be a very important clause. If, for any reason, any other gifts under your will are not able to completed, this clause takes effect. For example, if a beneficiary refuses to accept your gift or the chosen beneficiary has died and no alternate was selected or both the beneficiary and alternate has died, the gift is put back into your estate and would pass under the residuary clause. If there is no residuary clause included in your will, any property not disposed of under your will is treated as though you did not have a will and could potentially be forfeited to the state. To avoid this, it is strongly recommended that you make this clause mandatory in your will.

In addition, you may use this clause to give all of your estate (*except* your specific gifts) to one or more persons. For example: you make specific gifts of $1,000 to a sister and a car to a friend. By then naming your spouse as the residuary clause beneficiary, you will have gifted everything in your estate to your spouse--*except* the $1,000 and the car. You could then name your children, in equal shares, as the alternate residuary beneficiaries. In this manner, if your spouse were to die first, your children would then equally share your entire estate--*except* the $1,000 and the car.

Be sure to clearly identify the beneficiary and alternate beneficiary by full name. You can also name joint beneficiaries, such as several children, if you choose. The space provided for an identification of the relationship of the beneficiary can be simply a descriptive phrase like "my wife", or "my brother-in-law", or "my best friend". It does not mean that the beneficiary must be related to you personally.

☐ I give all the rest of my property, whether real or personal, wherever located, to _____,
                              [name of beneficiary]

my _____, or if not surviving
        [relationship of beneficiary]

to _____,
      [name of alternate beneficiary]

my _____.
        [relationship of alternate beneficiary]

Debt Forgiveness Clause

Optional: You may use this clause to forgive any debts owed to you personally. You should provide a clear description of the amount and nature of the debt being forgiven. You should also be certain to provide the full name and address of the debtor.

Be aware, however, that if you are married and the debt is owed to you and your spouse jointly, you may not legally be able to forgive the debt. On joint debts which you may wish to forgive, you are advised to consult an attorney.

If used, number this clause consecutively.

☐ I fully forgive the following debt(s) which are owed to me:

_____
[Description of debt]
_____
[Full name of debtor]
_____
[Address of debtor]
_____

_____
[Description of debt]
_____
[Full name of debtor]
_____
[Address of debtor]
_____

_____
[Description of debt]
_____
[Full name of debtor]
_____
[Address of debtor]
_____

Survivorship Clause

Mandatory: This clause should be included in every will. Number it consecutively. This clause provides for two possibilities. First, it provides for a required period of survival for any beneficiary to receive a gift under your will. The practical effect of this is to be certain that your property passes under your will and not that of a beneficiary who dies shortly after receiving your gift. The second portion of this clause provides for a determination of how your property should pass in the eventuality that both you and a beneficiary (most likely your spouse) should die in a manner that makes it impossible to determine who died first.

Without this clause in your will it would be possible that property would momentarily pass to a beneficiary under your will. When that person dies (possibly immediately if a result of a common accident or disaster) your property could wind up being left to the person whom your beneficiary designated, rather than to your alternate beneficiary.

If you and your spouse are both preparing wills, it is a good idea to be certain that each of your wills contains identical survivorship clauses. If you are each others primary beneficiary, it is also wise to attempt to coordinate who your alternate beneficiaries may be in the event of a simultaneous death.

☐ All beneficiaries named in this will must survive me by thirty days to receive any gift under this will.

If any beneficiary and I should die simultaneously, I shall be conclusively presumed to have survived that beneficiary for purposes of this will.

Disinheritance Clause

Optional: Use this clause to specifically disinherit anyone from receiving property under your will. It is much safer to specifically name the person to be disinherited than to rely upon simply not mentioning them in your will. To disinherit children and grandchildren of deceased children, they must be mentioned specifically. In the case of children born after a will is executed and of spouses of a marriage which takes place after a will is executed, there are differing provisions in many states as to the effect of their not being mentioned in a will. Please see the Appendix for information regarding the laws in your particular state. Another legal method to achieve approximately the same results as disinheritance is to leave the person a very small amount (at least $1.00) as a gift in your will. The safest method, however, is to specifically mention anyone to be disinherited and, also, to review your will each time there is a change in your family circumstances. Please see Chapter 12 for a discussion regarding changing your will.

Be sure to clearly identify the person being disinherited by full name. The space provided for an identification of the relationship of the executor can be simply a descriptive phrase like "my son", or "my brother".

If you do not wish to name anyone specifically, you may use the second clause as a general disinheritance clause. Do not use both clauses.

If either clause is used, number the clause consecutively.

☐ I specifically disinherit my _____,
                                         [relationship]

_____ ,
                    [name of person being disinherited]

of _____ ,
                 [address of person being disinherited]
and any other person not specifically named in this will.

☐ I intentionally disinherit any person not specifically named in this will.

Executor Clause

Mandatory: This clause must be included in every will. With this clause, you will make your choice of *executor*, the person who will administer and distribute your estate and an alternate choice if your first choice is unable to serve. A spouse, sibling, or other trusted party is usually chosen to act as executor. The person chosen should be a resident of the state in which you currently reside. Please refer back to Chapter 5 for more information regarding executors.

Note that you allow your executor to seek independent administration of your estate. Where allowed by state law, this enables your executor to manage your estate with minimal court supervision and can save your estate extensive court costs and legal fees. Additionally, you grant the executor broad powers to manage your estate and also provide that he or she not be required to post a bond in order to be appointed to serve as executor.

Be sure to clearly identify the executor and alternate executor by full name. The space provided for an identification of the relationship of the executor can be simply a descriptive phrase like "my wife", or "my brother-in-law", or "my best friend". It does not mean that the executor must be related to you personally.

You should number this clause consecutively.

☐ I appoint _____, my _____
              [full name of executor]   *[relationship]*

of _____, as Executor, to serve
           [address of executor]

without bond. If not surviving or otherwise unable to serve, I appoint

_____ , my _____
     [full name of alternate executor]   *[relationship]*

of _____, as Alternate
           [address of alternate executor]

Executor, also to serve without bond.

In addition to any powers, authority, and discretion granted by law, I grant such Executor or Alternate Executor any and all powers necessary to perform any acts, in his or her sole discretion and without court approval, for the management and distribution of my estate, including independent administration of my estate.

Guardianship Clause

Optional: With this clause you may designate your choice as to whom you wish to care for any of your minor children after you are gone. If you are married, your spouse is generally appointed by the probate or family court, regardless of your designation in a will. However, even if you are married, it is a good idea to choose your spouse as first choice and then provide a second choice. This will cover the contingency in which both you and your spouse die in a single accident.

Your choice should obviously be a trusted person whom you feel would provide the best care for your children in your absence. Be aware, however, that the court is guided, but not bound, by this particular choice in your will. The court's decision in appointing a child's guardian is based upon what would be in the best interests of the child. In most situations, however, a parent's choice as to who should be their child's guardian is almost universally followed by the courts. Be sure to clearly identify the guardian and alternate guardian by full name. The space provided for an identification of the relationship of the guardian can be simply a descriptive phrase like "my wife", or "my brother-in-law", or "my best friend". It does not mean that the guardian must be related to you personally. Additionally, you grant the guardian broad power to care for and manage your children's property and also provide that the appointed guardian not be required to post a bond in order to be appointed. If used, number this clause consecutively.

☐ If a Guardian is needed for any of my minor children, I appoint

_____, my _____,
[name of guardian]   [relationship]

of _____
                    [address of guardian]

as Guardian of the person(s) and property of my minor children, to serve without bond. If not surviving or unable to serve, I appoint

_____, my _____,
[name of alternate guardian]   [relationship]

of _____
                [address of alternate guardian]

as alternate Guardian, also to serve without bond.

In addition to any powers, authority, and discretion granted by law, I grant such Guardian or Alternate Guardian any and all powers to perform any acts, in his or her sole discretion and without court approval, for the management and distribution of the property of my minor children and for their care.

Children's Trust Fund Clause

Optional: It is with this clause that you may set up a Trust Fund for any gifts you have made to your minor children. You also may delay the time when they will actually have unrestricted control over your gift. It is not recommended, however, to attempt to delay receipt of control beyond the age of 30. If you have left assets to more than one child, this clause provides that separate individual trusts be set up for each child.

The choice for trustee under a children's trust should generally be the same person as you have chosen to be the children's guardian. This is not, however, a requirement. The choice of trustee is generally a spouse if alive, with the alternate being a trusted friend or family member. Be sure to clearly identify the trustee and alternate trustee by full name. The space provided for an identification of the relationship of the trustee can be simply a descriptive phrase like "my wife", or "my brother-in-law", or "my best friend". It does not mean that the trustee must be related to you personally.

The terms of the trust provide that the trustee may distribute any or all of the income or principal to the children as he or she deems necessary to provide for their health, support, and education. The trust will terminate when either the specific age is reached, all of the money is spent prior to that age, or the child dies prematurely. Upon termination, any remaining trust funds will be distributed to the child (beneficiary), if surviving; if not surviving, to the heirs of the beneficiary (if any), or to the residue of your estate. Additionally, you grant the trustee broad power to manage the trust and also provide that he or she not be required to post a bond in order to be appointed. Number this clause consecutively.

■ If any of my children are under _____ on my death, I
 [21, 25, or 30 years old]
direct that any property that I give them under this will be held in an individual trust for each child, under the following terms, until each shall reach

_____ .
[21, 25, or 30 years old]

A. I appoint _____, my _____,
 [name of trustee] [relationship]
of _____,
 [address of trustee]
as trustee of any and all required trusts, to serve without bond. If not surviving or otherwise unable to serve, then I appoint _____,
 [name of

_____, my _____,
 alternate trustee] [relationship]

---

of _____,
[address of alternate trustee]
as alternate Trustee, also to serve without bond. In addition to all powers, authority, and discretion granted by law, I grant such trustee or alternate trustee full power to perform any act, in his or her sole discretion and without court approval, to distribute and manage the assets of any such trust.

B.   In the trustee's sole discretion, the trustee may distribute any or all of the principal, income, or both as deemed necessary for the beneficiary's health, support, welfare, and education. Any income not distributed shall be added to the trust principal.

C.   Any such trust shall terminate when the beneficiary reaches the required age, when the beneficiary dies prior to reaching the required age, or when all trust funds have been distributed. Upon termination, any remaining undistributed principal and income shall pass to the beneficiary; or if not surviving, to the beneficiary's heirs; or if none, to the residue of my estate.

Organ Donation Clause

Optional: Use this clause to provide for any use of your body after death. You may, if you so desire, limit your donation to certain parts, for example, your eyes. If so desired, simply delete "any of my body parts and/or organs" from the following provision and insert your chosen donation. A copy of your will or instructions regarding this donation should be kept in a place which is readily-accessible by your executor and spouse. If used, number this clause consecutively.

☐ I declare that, pursuant to the Uniform Anatomical Gift Act, I donate any of my body parts and/or organs to any medical institution willing to accept them, and I direct my executor to carry out such donation.

Funeral and Burial Arrangements Clause

Optional: Use this clause to make known your wishes as to funeral and burial arrangements. Since it may be difficult to obtain your will quickly in an emergency, it is also a good idea to leave information regarding these desires with your executor, your spouse, or a close friend or relative. Number this clause consecutively.

☐ Funeral arrangements have been made with _____,
[name of funeral service]
of _____ for burial at
[address of funeral service]
_____, located in
[name of cemetery]
_____
[address of cemetery]
and I direct my Executor to carry out such arrangements.

Cremation Arrangements Clause

Optional: Use this clause to make known your wishes as to any cremation arrangements. It is also a good idea to leave information regarding these desires with your spouse or a close friend or relative, in as much as it may be difficult to obtain your will quickly in an emergency. Number this clause consecutively.

☐ Cremation arrangements have been made with _____,
[name of crematorium]
of _____
[address of crematorium]
and I direct my Executor to carry out such arrangements.

Signature and Witness Clauses

Mandatory: All of the following remaining portions of your will are mandatory and must be included in your will. Do not number any of these provisions. You will fill in the number of pages and the appropriate dates where indicated after you have properly typed or had your will typed.

I publish and sign this Last Will and Testament, consisting of _____ typewritten pages, on _____, 19 _____, and declare that I do so freely, for the purposes expressed, under no constraint or undue influence, and that I am of sound mind and of legal age.

_____
Signature of Testator

_____
Printed name of Testator

On _____, 19 _____, in the presence of all of us, the above-named Testator published and signed this Last Will and Testament, and then at Testator's request, and in Testator's presence, and in each other's presence, we all signed below as witnesses, and we declare, under penalty of perjury, that, to the best of our knowledge, the Testator signed this instrument freely, under no constraint or undue influence, and is of sound mind and legal age.

_____
Signature of Witness

_____
Printed name of Witness

_____
Address of Witness

_____

Signature of Witness

_____

Printed name of Witness

_____

Address of Witness

_____

Signature of Witness

_____

Printed name of Witness

_____

Address of Witness

Self-Proving Affidavit

Although use of this clause is not a strict legal necessity, it is strongly recommended that you prepare and use this Affidavit with all wills. Although a few states have not enacted legislation to allow for their use in court, the current trend is for all courts to allow their use. This Affidavit will allow for your signature on your will to be proved without the necessity of having the three witnesses appear in court, a point which will save time, money, and trouble in having your will admitted to probate when necessary.

SELF-PROVING AFFIDAVIT

We, the undersigned Testator and witnesses, being first sworn on oath and under penalty of perjury, state that, in the presence of all the witnesses, the Testator published and signed the above Last Will and Testament and then, at Testator's request, and in the presence of the Testator and of each other, each of the witnesses signed as witnesses, and that, to the best of our knowledge, the Testator signed said Last Will and Testament freely, under no constraint or undue influence, and is of sound mind and legal age.

_____
Signature of Testator

_____
Printed name of Testator

_____
Signature of Witness

_____
Printed name of Witness

_____
Address of Witness

_____
Signature of Witness

_____
Printed name of Witness

_____
Address of Witness

_____
Signature of Witness

_____
Printed name of Witness

_____
Address of Witness

County of _____}   SS.
State of _____}

Subscribed, sworn to, and acknowledged before me on _____,
19_____ by _____, the Testator, and
          [full name of testator]

by _____,
      [full name of first witness]

_____,
      [full name of second witness]

_____,
      [full name of third witness]
the Witnesses.

_____
Signature of Notary Public

_____
Printed name of Notary Public

Notary Public,
In and for the County of _____,
State of _____.

Chapter 7

Pre-assembled Wills

In this chapter are contained four separate wills which have been prepared for certain general situations using the will clauses in Chapter 6. They are no different than wills which may be prepared by assembling a will yourself from separate clauses. These wills are presented for the purpose of allowing persons whose situations fall into certain standard formats to prepare their wills quickly and easily on pre-assembled forms. The wills in this chapter, however, do not have certain provisions which may be included in wills which are custom-prepared using the will clauses in Chapter 6. None of the wills in this chapter have the following clauses:

      ☒   Entire Estate Gift Clause
      ☒   Debt Forgiveness Clause
      ☒   Disinheritance Clause
      ☒   Organ Donation Clause
      ☒   Funeral Arrangements Clause
      ☒   Cremation Arrangements Clause

If you wish for your will to contain any of these clauses, you should prepare a will using the instructions contained in Chapter 6. For those of you who do not desire to use any of the above clauses, the use of one of the wills in this chapter may be appropriate. Please read the description prior to each will to be certain that the will you chose is appropriate in your particular situation.

Instructions

These pre-assembled will forms are intended to be used as simplified worksheets in preparing your own personal will. They should be filled-in by hand and then re-typed according to the following instructions and the instructions contained in Chapter 9. These pre-assembled wills are *not* intended to be filled-in and used "as is" as an original will. Such use would most likely result in an invalid will. They must be re-typed. Be certain to carefully follow all of the instructions for use of these forms. They are not difficult to fill out, but must be prepared properly to be legally valid. In order to prepare any of the wills in this chapter, you should follow these simple steps:

1.   Carefully read through all of the clauses in the blank pre-assembled will to determine if the clauses provided are suitable in your situation. Choose the will that is most appropriate. Make a photo-copy of the will that you choose to use as a worksheet. If you wish, you may use this book itself as a worksheet (unless it is a library book!)

2.   Using your Property and Beneficiary Questionnaires, fill in the appropriate information where necessary on these forms. As you fill in the information for each clause, keep in mind the following instructions:

   ❑   **Title Clause**: The title clause is *mandatory* for all wills and must be included. Fill in the name blank with your full legal name. If you have been known under more than one name, use your principal name. Do not number this title.

   ❑   **Identification Clause**: The identification clause is *mandatory* and must be included in all wills. Do not number this clause. In the first blank, include any other names which you are known by. Do this by adding the phrase: "also known as" after your principal full name. For example: *John James Smith, also known as Jimmy John Smith*. In the spaces provided for your residence, use the location of your principal residence; where you currently live permanently.

   ❑   **Marital Status Clause**: Each of the pre-assembled clauses in this chapter are for a specific marital status situation. Select the proper will and fill in the appropriate information in this clause. This clause will always be numbered #1.

   ❑   **Identification of Children Clause**: This clause will only be present in the pre-assembled wills which relate to children. In this clause, you should specifically identify all of your children, indicating their names, current addresses, and dates of birth. Cross out those spaces which are not used. Number this clause consecutively, if used.

❑ **Identification of Grandchildren Clause**: This clause will only be used in the pre-assembled wills which relate to children. If you do not have grandchildren, cross out this entire clause and re-number the following clauses accordingly. If you do have grandchildren, in this clause you should specifically identify all of your grandchildren, indicating their names, current addresses, and dates of birth. Cross out those spaces which are not used. Number this clause consecutively, if used.

❑ **Specific Gifts Clause**: For making specific gifts, use as many of the "I give . . ." paragraphs as is necessary to complete your chosen gifts. In these paragraphs, you may make any type of gift that you wish, either a cash gift, a gift of a specific piece of personal property or real estate, or a specific share of your total estate. If you wish to give some of your estate in the form of portions of the total, it is recommended to use fractional portions. For example, if you wish to leave your estate in equal shares to two persons, use "I give one-half of my total estate to . . . " for each party. Although none of the wills in this chapter contain a specific clause which states that you give one person your entire estate, you may make such a gift using this clause by simply stating: "I give my entire estate to ..." Be sure that you do not attempt to give any other gifts. However, you should still include the residuary clause in your will, which is explained below.

In your description of the property, you should be as specific and precise as possible. For land, it is suggested that you use the description exactly as shown on the deed to the property. For personal property, be certain that your description clearly differentiates your gift from any other property. For example: "I give my blue velvet coat which was a gift from my brother John to . . . ". Use serial numbers, colors, or any other descriptive words to clearly indicate the exact nature of the gift. For cash gifts, specifically indicate the amount of the gift. For gifts of securities, state the amount of shares and the name of the company. You may add simple conditions to the gifts that you make, if you desire. For example: You may state "I give $1,000 to the Centerville Church for use in purchasing a new roof for the church". Complex conditions, however, are not possible in this clause, and immoral or illegal conditions are not acceptable.

Be sure to clearly identify the beneficiary and alternate beneficiary by full name. You can also name joint beneficiaries, such as several children, if you choose. The space provided for an identification of the relationship of the beneficiary can be simply a descriptive phrase like "my wife", or "my brother-in-law", or "my best friend". It does not mean that the beneficiary must be related to you personally.

The choice of alternate beneficiary is for the purpose of allowing you to designate someone to receive the gift if your first choice to receive the gift dies before you do (or, in the case of a organization chosen as primary beneficiary, is no longer in business). In this or any of the other gift clauses, your choice for alternate beneficiary may be one or more persons or an organization. It is recommended to always specifically name your beneficiary(s), rather than using a description only, such as "my children". In addition, you may delete the alternate beneficiary choice and substitute the words "the residue" instead. The result of this change will be that if your primary beneficiary dies before you do, your gift to pass under your residuary clause, which is discussed below. If additional gifts are desired, simply photo-copy an additional page.

❑ **Residuary Clause**: Although not a technical legal requirement, it is strongly recommended that you include the residuary clause in every will. With it, you will choose the person, persons, or organization to receive anything not covered by other clauses of your will. Even if you feel that you have given away everything that you own under other clauses of your will, this can be a very important clause.

If, for any reason, any other gifts under your will are not able to completed, this clause goes into effect. For example, if a beneficiary refuses to accept your gift or the chosen beneficiary has died and no alternate was selected or both the beneficiary and alternate has died, the gift is put back into your estate and would pass under the residuary clause. If there is no residuary clause included in your will, any property not disposed of under your will is treated as though you did not have a will and could potentially be forfeited to the state. To avoid this, it is strongly recommended that you make this clause mandatory in your will.

In addition, you may use this clause to give all of your estate (*except* your specific gifts) to one or more persons. For example: you make specific gifts of $1,000 to a sister and a car to a friend. By then naming your spouse as the residuary clause beneficiary, you will have gifted everything in your estate to your spouse--*except* the $1,000 and the car. You could then name your children, in equal shares, as the alternate residuary beneficiaries. In this manner, if your spouse were to die first, your children would then equally share your entire estate--*except* the $1,000 and the car.

Be sure to clearly identify the beneficiary by full name. The space provided for an identification of the relationship of the beneficiary can be simply a descriptive phrase like "my wife", or "my brother-in-law", or "my best friend". It does not mean that the beneficiary must be related to you personally.

❑ **Survivorship Clause**: This clause should be included in every will. This clause provides for two possibilities. First, it provides for a required period of survival for any beneficiary to receive a gift under your will. The practical effect of this is to be certain that your property passes under your will and not that of a beneficiary who dies shortly after receiving your gift. The second portion of this clause provides for a determination of how your property should pass in the eventuality that both you and a beneficiary (most likely your spouse) should die in a manner that makes it impossible to determine who died first.

Without this clause in your will it would be possible that property would momentarily pass to a beneficiary under your will. When that person dies (possibly immediately if a result of a common accident or disaster) your property could wind up being left to the person whom your beneficiary designated, rather than to your alternate beneficiary.

If you and your spouse are both preparing wills, it is a good idea to be certain that each of your wills contains identical survivorship clauses. If you are each others primary beneficiary, it is also wise to attempt to coordinate who your alternate beneficiaries may be in the event of a simultaneous death.

❑ **Executor Clause**: The executor clause must be included in every will. With this clause, you will make your choice of *executor*, the person who will administer and distribute your estate and an alternate choice if your first choice is unable to serve. A spouse, sibling, or other trusted party is usually chosen to act as executor. The person chosen should be a resident of the state in which you currently reside. Please refer to Chapter 5 for more information on executors.

Note that you allow your executor to seek independent administration of your estate. Where allowed by state law, this enables your executor to manage your estate with minimal court supervision and can save your estate extensive court costs and legal fees. Additionally, you grant the executor broad powers to manage your estate and also provide that he or she not be required to post a bond in order to be appointed to serve as executor.

Be sure to clearly identify the executor and alternate executor by full name. The space provided for an identification of the relationship of the executor can be simply a descriptive phrase like "my wife", or "my brother-in-law", or "my best friend". It does not mean that the executor must be related to you personally.

❑ **Child Guardianship Clause**: This clause will only be present in the pre-assembled wills which relate to children. With this clause you may designate your choice as to whom you wish to care for any of your minor children after you are gone. If you are married, your spouse is generally appointed by the probate or family court, regardless of your designation in a will. However, even if you are married, it is a good idea to choose your spouse as first choice and then provide a second choice. This will cover the contingency in which both you and your spouse die in a single accident.

Your choice should obviously be a trusted person whom you feel would provide the best care for your children in your absence. Be aware, however, that the court is guided, but not bound, by this particular choice in your will. The court's decision in appointing a child's guardian is based upon what would be in the best interests of the child. In most situations, however, a parent's choice as to who should be their child's guardian is almost universally followed by the courts. Additionally, you grant the guardian broad power to care for and manage your children's property and also provide that the appointed guardian not be required to post a bond in order to be appointed.

Be sure to clearly identify the guardian and alternate guardian by full name. The space provided for an identification of the relationship of the guardian can be simply a descriptive phrase like "my wife", or "my brother-in-law", or "my best friend". It does not mean that the guardian must be related to you personally.

❑ **Children's Trust Fund Clause**: This clause will only be present in the pre-assembled wills which relate to children. It is with this clause that you may set up a Trust Fund for any gifts you have made to your minor children. You also may delay the time when they will actually have unrestricted control over your gift. It is not recommended, however, to attempt to delay receipt of control beyond the age of 30. If you have left assets to more than one child, this clause provides that individual trusts be set up for each child.

The choice for trustee under a children's trust should generally be the same person as you have chosen to be the children's guardian. This is not, however, a requirement. The choice of trustee is generally a spouse if alive, with the alternate being a trusted friend or family member. Be sure to clearly identify the trustee and alternate trustee by full name. The space provided for an identification of the relationship of the trustee can be simply a descriptive phrase like "my wife", or "my brother-in-law", or "my best friend". It does not mean that the trustee must be related to you personally.

The terms of the trust provide that the trustee may distribute any or all of the income or principal to the children as he or she deems necessary to provide for their health, support, and education. The trust will terminate when either the specific age is reached, all of the money is spent prior to that age, or the child dies prematurely. Upon termination, any remaining trust funds will be distributed to the child (beneficiary), if surviving; if not surviving, to the heirs of the beneficiary (if any); or if there are none, to the residue of your estate. Additionally, you grant the trustee broad power to manage the trust and also provide that he or she not be required to post a bond in order to be appointed.

❑ **Signature Clause**: The signature lines and final paragraph of your will are mandatory and must be included in your will. Do not number any of these provisions. You will fill in the number of pages and the appropriate dates where indicated after you have properly typed or had your will typed.

3.   After you have filled in all of the appropriate information, carefully re-read your entire will. Be certain that it contains all of the correct information that you desire. Then starting at the beginning of the will, cross out all of the words and phrases in the pre-assembled will that do not apply in your situation. All of the identification lines under the blanks should also be crossed out as you will not be typing them on your final will.

4.   After all of the extraneous information has been crossed out, number each clause that you will be using in the box provided before each clause. The first marital status clause in each will has been numbered #1 already, so the next clause in your will should begin with #2. Do not number the signature clause at the end of your will.

5.   When you have completed numbering all of your will clauses, look over the sample wills in the next chapter to see how a completed will should look. Then, turn to Chapter 9 for instructions on typing and final preparation of your will.

6.   For any of these pre-assembled wills that you decide to prepare, a Self-Proving Affidavit should also be prepared. Please consult the information and form for the Affidavit that is provided at the end of Chapter 6. Please fill in the appropriate blanks in the Self-Proving Affidavit form and prepare and sign it as instructed in Chapters 9 and 10.

Will for Married Person with Children (using Children's Trust)

This will is appropriate for use by a married person with one or more minor children, who desires to place the property and assets which may be left to the children in a trust fund. In addition, this will allows the parent to chooses a person to act as guardian for the child or children. In most cases, a married person may desire to chose the other spouse as both trustee and guardian for any of their children, although this is not a legal requirement. Each spouse/parent must prepare their own will. ***Do not*** attempt to prepare a joint will for both of you together.

This will contains the following standard clauses:

- ❑ Title Clause
- ❑ Identification Clause
- ❑ Marital Status Clauses
- ❑ Children Identification Clause
- ❑ Grandchildren Identification Clause
- ❑ Specific Gifts Clause
- ❑ Residuary Clause
- ❑ Survivorship Clause
- ❑ Executor Clause
- ❑ Guardianship Clause
- ❑ Children's Trust Fund Clause
- ❑ Signature and Witness Clause

This will ***does not*** contain these following clauses:

- ☒ Entire Estate Gift Clause
- ☒ Debt Forgiveness Clause
- ☒ Disinheritance Clause
- ☒ Organ Donation Clause
- ☒ Funeral Arrangements Clause
- ☒ Cremation Arrangements Clause

Fill in each of the appropriate blanks in this will using the information which you included in your Property and Beneficiary Questionnaires. Cross out any information that is not appropriate to your situation.

Last Will and Testament of _____
[your full name]

I, _____, a resident
[your full name and any other names that you have used]

of _____, _____,
[name of city or town]   [name of county]

_____, declare that this is my
[name of state]

Last Will and Testament and I revoke all previous wills and codicils.

1.   I am married to _____.
[spouse's full name]

☐ I was previously married to _____.
[previous spouse's full name]

That marriage ended on _____, 19 _____,
[date]

by _____.
[death, divorce, or annulment]

☐ I have _____children living. Their names, addresses, and
[number of children]

dates of birth are as follows:

_____
[Child's name]

_____
[Child's address]

_____
[Child's date of birth]

_____
[Child's name]

_____
[Child's address]

_____

_____
[Child's date of birth]

_____
[Child's name]

_____
[Child's address]

_____

_____
[Child's date of birth]

_____
[Child's name]

_____
[Child's address]

_____

_____
[Child's date of birth]

_____
[Child's name]

_____
[Child's address]

_____

_____
[Child's date of birth]

☐ I have _____ grandchildren living. Their names,
[number of Grandchildren]
addresses, and dates of birth are as follows:

_____
[Grandchild's name]

_____
[Grandchild's address]

_____

_____
[Grandchild's date of birth]

_____
[Grandchild's name]

_____
[Grandchild's address]

_____

_____
[Grandchild's date of birth]

_____
[Grandchild's name]

_____
[Grandchild's address]

_____

_____
[Grandchild's date of birth]

_____
[Grandchild's name]

_____
[Grandchild's address]

_____

_____
[Grandchild's date of birth]

_____
[Grandchild's name]

_____
[Grandchild's address]

_____

_____
[Grandchild's date of birth]

☐ I make the following specific gifts:

I give _____

_____
[complete description of property]

to _____
[name of beneficiary]   ,

my _____
[relationship of beneficiary]   , or if not surviving

to_____
[name of alternate beneficiary]   ,

my _____
[relationship of alternate beneficiary]   .

I give _____

_____
[complete description of property]

to _____
[name of beneficiary]   ,

my _____
[relationship of beneficiary]   , or if not surviving

to_____
[name of alternate beneficiary]   ,

my _____
[relationship of alternate beneficiary]   .

I give _____

_____
          [complete description of property]

to _____ ,
          [name of beneficiary]

my _____ , or if not surviving
          [relationship of beneficiary]

to _____ ,
          [name of alternate beneficiary]

my _____ .
          [relationship of alternate beneficiary]

I give _____

_____
          [complete description of property]

to _____ ,
          [name of beneficiary]

my _____ , or if not surviving
          [relationship of beneficiary]

to _____ ,
          [name of alternate beneficiary]

my _____ .
          [relationship of alternate beneficiary]

I give _____

_____
          [complete description of property]

to _____ ,
          [name of beneficiary]

my _____ , or if not surviving
          [relationship of beneficiary]

to _____ ,
          [name of alternate beneficiary]

my _____ .
          [relationship of alternate beneficiary]

☐ I give all the rest of my property, whether real or personal, wherever located, to _____,
_____
[name of beneficiary]

my _____, or if not
_____
[relationship of beneficiary]

surviving to_____,
_____
[name of alternate beneficiary]

my _____.
_____
[relationship of alternate beneficiary]

☐ All beneficiaries named in this will must survive me by thirty days to receive any gift under this will.

If any beneficiary and I should die simultaneously, I shall be conclusively presumed to have survived that beneficiary for purposes of this will.

☐ I appoint _____, my _____
_____   _____
[full name of executor]   [relationship]

of _____, as Executor, to serve
_____
[address of executor]

without bond. If not surviving or otherwise unable to serve, I appoint

_____, my _____
_____   _____
[full name of alternate executor]   [relationship]

of _____, as Alternate
_____
[address of alternate executor]

Executor, also to serve without bond.

In addition to any powers, authority, and discretion granted by law, I grant such Executor or Alternate Executor any and all powers to perform any acts, in his or her sole discretion and without court approval, for the management and distribution of my estate, including independent administration of my estate.

☐ If a Guardian is needed for any of my minor children, I appoint
_____, my _____,
_____   _____
[name of guardian]   [relationship]

of _____
_____
[address of guardian]

as Guardian of the person(s) and property of my minor children, to serve without bond. If not surviving or unable to serve, I appoint

_____, my _____,
[name of alternate guardian]   [relationship]
of _____
            [address of alternate guardian]
as alternate Guardian, also to serve without bond.

In addition to any powers, authority, and discretion granted by law, I grant such Guardian or Alternate Guardian any and all powers to perform any acts, in his or her sole discretion and without court approval, for the management and distribution of the property of my minor children.

☐ If any of my children are under _____ on my death, I
                                              [21, 25, or 30 years old]
direct that any property that I give them under this will be held in an individual trust for each child, under the following terms, until each shall reach

_____.
[21, 25, or 30 years old]

   A.   I appoint _____, my _____,
                          [name of trustee]   [relationship]
         of _____,
                     [address of trustee]
as trustee of any and all required trusts, to serve without bond. If not surviving or otherwise unable to serve, then I appoint _____,
                                                                   [name of
_____, my _____,
   alternate trustee]   [relationship]
         of _____,
                  [address of alternate trustee]
as alternate Trustee, also to serve without bond. In addition to all powers, authority, and discretion granted by law, I grant such trustee or alternate trustee full power to perform any act, in his or her sole discretion and without court approval, to distribute and manage the assets of any such trust.

   B.   In the trustee's sole discretion, the trustee may distribute any or all of the principal, income, or both as deemed necessary for the beneficiary's health, support, welfare, and education. Any income not distributed shall be added to the trust principal.

   C.   Any such trust shall terminate when the beneficiary reaches the required age, when the beneficiary dies prior to reaching the required age, or when all trust funds have been distributed. Upon termination, any remaining undistributed principal and income shall pass to the beneficiary; or if not surviving, to the beneficiary's heirs; or if none, to the residue of my estate.

I publish and sign this Last Will and Testament, consisting of _____ typewritten pages, on _____, 19 _____, and declare that I do so freely, for the purposes expressed, under no constraint or undue influence, and that I am of sound mind and of legal age.

_____
Signature of Testator

_____
Printed name of Testator

On _____, 19 _____, in the presence of all of us, the above-named Testator published and signed this Last Will and Testament, and then at Testator's request, and in Testator's presence, and in each other's presence, we all signed below as witnesses, and we declare, under penalty of perjury, that, to the best of our knowledge, the Testator signed this instrument freely, under no constraint or undue influence, and is of sound mind and legal age.

_____
Signature of Witness

_____
Printed name of Witness

_____
Address of Witness

_____

Signature of Witness

_____

Printed name of Witness

_____

Address of Witness

_____

Signature of Witness

_____

Printed name of Witness

_____

Address of Witness

Will for Married Person with No Children

This will is appropriate for use by a married person with no children or grandchildren. It allows for a married person to make specific gifts of property to any persons or organizations that they have chosen and to choose an executor.

This will contains the following standard clauses:

- ❑ Title Clause
- ❑ Identification Clause
- ❑ Marital Status Clauses
- ❑ Specific Gifts Clause
- ❑ Residuary Clause
- ❑ Survivorship Clause
- ❑ Executor Clause
- ❑ Signature and Witness Clause

This will *does not* contain these following clauses:

- ☒ Children Identification Clause
- ☒ Grandchildren Identification Clause
- ☒ Entire Estate Gift Clause
- ☒ Debt Forgiveness Clause
- ☒ Disinheritance Clause
- ☒ Guardianship Clause
- ☒ Children's Trust Fund Clause
- ☒ Organ Donation Clause
- ☒ Funeral Arrangements Clause
- ☒ Cremation Arrangements Clause

Fill in each of the appropriate blanks in this will using the information which you included in your Property and Beneficiary Questionnaires. Cross out any information that you do not use and number each clause consecutively.

Last Will and Testament of _____
[your full name]

I, _____, a resident

[your full name and any other names that you have used]

of _____, _____,

[name of city or town]   [name of county]

_____, declare that this is my

[name of state]

Last Will and Testament and I revoke all previous wills and codicils.

1.   I am married to _____.

[spouse's full name]

☐ I was previously married to _____.

[previous spouse's full name]

That marriage ended on _____, 19 _____,

[date]

by _____.

[death, divorce, or annulment]

☐ I have no children or grandchildren living.

☐ I make the following specific gifts:

I give _____

_____

[complete description of property]

to _____,

[name of beneficiary]

my _____, or if not surviving

[relationship of beneficiary]

to_____,

[name of alternate beneficiary]

my _____.

[relationship of alternate beneficiary]

I give _____

_____
        [complete description of property]

to _____,
        [name of beneficiary]

my _____, or if not surviving
        [relationship of beneficiary]

to_____,
        [name of alternate beneficiary]

my _____.
        [relationship of alternate beneficiary]

I give _____

_____
        [complete description of property]

to _____,
        [name of beneficiary]

my _____, or if not surviving
        [relationship of beneficiary]

to_____,
        [name of alternate beneficiary]

my _____.
        [relationship of alternate beneficiary]

I give _____

_____
        [complete description of property]

to _____,
        [name of beneficiary]

my _____, or if not surviving
        [relationship of beneficiary]

to_____,
        [name of alternate beneficiary]

my _____.
        [relationship of alternate beneficiary]

I give _____

_____
         [complete description of property]

to _____,
       [name of beneficiary]

my _____, or if not surviving
       [relationship of beneficiary]

to_____,
       [name of alternate beneficiary]

my _____.
       [relationship of alternate beneficiary]

I give _____

_____
         [complete description of property]

to _____,
       [name of beneficiary]

my _____, or if not surviving
       [relationship of beneficiary]

to_____,
       [name of alternate beneficiary]

my _____.
       [relationship of alternate beneficiary]

☐ I give all the rest of my property, whether real or personal, wherever located, to _____,
             [name of beneficiary]

my _____, or if not
       [relationship of beneficiary]

surviving to_____,
              [name of alternate beneficiary]

my _____.
    [relationship of alternate beneficiary]

☐ All beneficiaries named in this will must survive me by thirty days to receive any gift under this will.

If any beneficiary and I should die simultaneously, I shall be conclusively presumed to have survived that beneficiary for purposes of this will.

☐ I appoint _____, my _____
[full name of executor]   [relationship]

of _____, as Executor, to serve
[address of executor]

without bond. If not surviving or otherwise unable to serve, I appoint

_____ , my _____
[full name of alternate executor]   [relationship]

of _____, as Alternate
[address of alternate executor]

Executor, also to serve without bond.

In addition to any powers, authority, and discretion granted by law, I grant such Executor or Alternate Executor any and all powers to perform any acts, in his or her sole discretion and without court approval, for the management and distribution of my estate, including independent administration of my estate.

I publish and sign this Last Will and Testament, consisting of _____ typewritten pages, on _____, 19 _____, and declare that I do so freely, for the purposes expressed, under no constraint or undue influence, and that I am of sound mind and of legal age.

_____
Signature of Testator

_____
Printed name of Testator

On _____, 19 _____, in the presence of all of us, the above-named Testator published and signed this Last Will and Testament, and then at Testator's request, and in Testator's presence, and in each other's presence, we all signed below as witnesses, and we declare, under penalty of perjury, that, to the best of our knowledge, the Testator signed this instrument freely, under no constraint or undue influence, and is of sound mind and legal age.

_____
Signature of Witness

_____
Printed name of Witness

_____
Address of Witness

_____
Signature of Witness

_____
Printed name of Witness

_____
Address of Witness

_____
Signature of Witness

_____
Printed name of Witness

_____
Address of Witness

Will for Single Person with No Children

This will is appropriate for use by a single person with no children or grandchildren. It allows for a single person to make specific gifts of property to any persons or organizations that they have chosen and to choose an executor. It should only be used by a single person who has never been previously married. If you are presently single, but were previously married, please prepare your will using the instructions provided in Chapter 6.

This will contains the following standard clauses:

- ❏ Title Clause
- ❏ Identification Clause
- ❏ Marital Status Clauses
- ❏ Specific Gifts Clause
- ❏ Residuary Clause
- ❏ Survivorship Clause
- ❏ Executor Clause
- ❏ Signature and Witness Clause

This will *does not* contain these following clauses:

- ☒ Children Identification Clause
- ☒ Grandchildren Identification Clause
- ☒ Entire Estate Gift Clause
- ☒ Debt Forgiveness Clause
- ☒ Disinheritance Clause
- ☒ Guardianship Clause
- ☒ Children's Trust Fund Clause
- ☒ Organ Donation Clause
- ☒ Funeral Arrangements Clause
- ☒ Cremation Arrangements Clause

Fill in each of the appropriate blanks in this will using the information which you included in your Property and Beneficiary Questionnaires. Cross out any information that you do not use and number each clause consecutively.

Last Will and Testament of _____
                                   [your full name]

I, _____, a resident
              [your full name and any other names that you have used]
of _____, _____,
         [name of city or town]   [name of county]
_____, declare that this is my
              [name of state]
Last Will and Testament and I revoke all previous wills and codicils.

1.   I have never been married and I have no children or grandchildren.

☐ I make the following specific gifts:

I give _____

_____
              [complete description of property]
to _____,
              [name of beneficiary]
my _____, or if not surviving
              [relationship of beneficiary]
to_____,
              [name of alternate beneficiary]
my _____.
              [relationship of alternate beneficiary]

I give _____

_____
              [complete description of property]
to _____,
              [name of beneficiary]
my _____, or if not surviving
              [relationship of beneficiary]
to_____,
              [name of alternate beneficiary]
my _____.
              [relationship of alternate beneficiary]

I give _____

_____
           [complete description of property]

to _____,
       [name of beneficiary]

my _____, or if not surviving
       [relationship of beneficiary]

to_____,
      [name of alternate beneficiary]

my _____.
       [relationship of alternate beneficiary]

I give _____

_____
           [complete description of property]

to _____,
       [name of beneficiary]

my _____, or if not surviving
       [relationship of beneficiary]

to_____,
      [name of alternate beneficiary]

my _____.
       [relationship of alternate beneficiary]

I give _____

_____
           [complete description of property]

to _____,
       [name of beneficiary]

my _____, or if not surviving
       [relationship of beneficiary]

to_____,
      [name of alternate beneficiary]

my _____.
       [relationship of alternate beneficiary]

I give _____

_____
                     [complete description of property]
to _____,
               [name of beneficiary]
my _____, or if not surviving
           [relationship of beneficiary]
to_____,
            [name of alternate beneficiary]
my _____.
           [relationship of alternate beneficiary]

☐ I give all the rest of my property, whether real or personal, wherever located, to _____,
                      [name of beneficiary]
my _____, or if not
           [relationship of beneficiary]
surviving to_____,
                 [name of alternate beneficiary]
my _____.
           [relationship of alternate beneficiary]

☐ All beneficiaries named in this will must survive me by thirty days to receive any gift under this will.

If any beneficiary and I should die simultaneously, I shall be conclusively presumed to have survived that beneficiary for purposes of this will.

☐ I appoint _____, my _____
             [full name of executor]   *[relationship]*
of _____, as Executor, to serve
            [address of executor]
without bond. If not surviving or otherwise unable to serve, I appoint
_____ , my _____
       [full name of alternate executor]   *[relationship]*
of _____, as Alternate
            [address of alternate executor]
Executor, also to serve without bond.

In addition to any powers, authority, and discretion granted by law, I grant such Executor or Alternate Executor any and all powers to perform any acts, in his or her sole discretion and without court approval, for the management and distribution of my estate, including independent administration of my estate.

I publish and sign this Last Will and Testament, consisting of _____ typewritten pages, on _____, 19 _____, and declare that I do so freely, for the purposes expressed, under no constraint or undue influence, and that I am of sound mind and of legal age.

_____
Signature of Testator

_____
Printed name of Testator

On _____, 19 _____, in the presence of all of us, the above-named Testator published and signed this Last Will and Testament, and then at Testator's request, and in Testator's presence, and in each other's presence, we all signed below as witnesses, and we declare, under penalty of perjury, that, to the best of our knowledge, the Testator signed this instrument freely, under no constraint or undue influence, and is of sound mind and legal age.

_____
Signature of Witness

_____
Printed name of Witness

_____
Address of Witness

_____

Signature of Witness

_____

Printed name of Witness

_____

Address of Witness

_____

Signature of Witness

_____

Printed name of Witness

_____

Address of Witness

Will for Single Person with Children (using Children's Trust)

This will is appropriate for use by a single person with one or more minor children (or with grandchildren), who desires to place the property and assets which may be left to the children in a trust fund. In addition, this will allows the parent to chooses a person to act as guardian for the child or children. In most cases, a person may desire to chose the other parent as both trustee and guardian for any of their children, although this is not a legal requirement. Each parent must prepare their own will.

This will contains the following standard clauses:

- ❑ Title Clause
- ❑ Identification Clause
- ❑ Marital Status Clauses
- ❑ Children Identification Clause
- ❑ Grandchildren Identification Clause
- ❑ Specific Gifts Clause
- ❑ Residuary Clause
- ❑ Survivorship Clause
- ❑ Executor Clause
- ❑ Guardianship Clause
- ❑ Children's Trust Fund Clause
- ❑ Signature and Witness Clause

This will *does not* contain these following clauses:

- ☒ Entire Estate Gift Clause
- ☒ Debt Forgiveness Clause
- ☒ Disinheritance Clause
- ☒ Organ Donation Clause
- ☒ Funeral Arrangements Clause
- ☒ Cremation Arrangements Clause

Fill in each of the appropriate blanks in this will using the information which you included in your Property and Beneficiary Questionnaires. Cross out any information that you do not use and number each clause consecutively.

Last Will and Testament of _____
[your full name]

I, _____, a resident
[your full name and any other names that you have used]
of _____, _____,
[name of city or town]   [name of county]
_____, declare that this is my
[name of state]
Last Will and Testament and I revoke all previous wills and codicils.

1.   I am not currently married. I was previously married to _____
[previous
_____. That marriage ended on _____,
spouse's full name]   [date]
19 _____, by _____.
[death, divorce, or annulment]

☐ I have _____children living. Their names, addresses, and
[number of children]
dates of birth are as follows:

_____
[Child's name]
_____
[Child's address]
_____
[Child's date of birth]

_____
[Child's name]
_____
[Child's address]
_____
[Child's date of birth]

_____
[Child's name]

_____
[Child's address]

_____

_____
[Child's date of birth]

_____
[Child's name]

_____
[Child's address]

_____

_____
[Child's date of birth]

_____
[Child's name]

_____
[Child's address]

_____

_____
[Child's date of birth]

_____
[Child's name]

_____
[Child's address]

_____

_____
[Child's date of birth]

☐ I have _____ grandchildren living. Their names,
[number of Grandchildren]
addresses, and dates of birth are as follows:

_____

[Grandchild's name]
_____

[Grandchild's address]
_____

_____

[Grandchild's date of birth]

_____

[Grandchild's name]
_____

[Grandchild's address]
_____

_____

[Grandchild's date of birth]

_____

[Grandchild's name]
_____

[Grandchild's address]
_____

_____

[Grandchild's date of birth]

_____

[Grandchild's name]
_____

[Grandchild's address]
_____

_____

[Grandchild's date of birth]

_____

_____[Grandchild's name]_____

_____[Grandchild's address]_____

_____

_____[Grandchild's date of birth]_____

_____

_____[Grandchild's name]_____

_____[Grandchild's address]_____

_____

_____[Grandchild's date of birth]_____

■ I make the following specific gifts:

I give _____

_____
          [complete description of property]

to _____,
          [name of beneficiary]

my _____, or if not surviving
          [relationship of beneficiary]

to_____,
          [name of alternate beneficiary]

my _____.
          [relationship of alternate beneficiary]

I give _____

_____
           [complete description of property]

to _____,
       [name of beneficiary]

my _____, or if not surviving
       [relationship of beneficiary]

to_____,
      [name of alternate beneficiary]

my _____.
       [relationship of alternate beneficiary]

I give _____

_____
           [complete description of property]

to _____,
       [name of beneficiary]

my _____, or if not surviving
       [relationship of beneficiary]

to_____,
      [name of alternate beneficiary]

my _____.
       [relationship of alternate beneficiary]

I give _____

_____
           [complete description of property]

to _____,
       [name of beneficiary]

my _____, or if not surviving
       [relationship of beneficiary]

to_____,
      [name of alternate beneficiary]

my _____.
       [relationship of alternate beneficiary]

I give _____

_____
               [complete description of property]

to _____,
               [name of beneficiary]

my _____, or if not surviving
               [relationship of beneficiary]

to_____,
               [name of alternate beneficiary]

my _____.
               [relationship of alternate beneficiary]

☐ I give all the rest of my property, whether real or personal, wherever located, to _____,
               [name of beneficiary]

my _____, or if not
               [relationship of beneficiary]

surviving to_____,
               [name of alternate beneficiary]

my _____.
               [relationship of alternate beneficiary]

☐ All beneficiaries named in this will must survive me by thirty days to receive any gift under this will.

If any beneficiary and I should die simultaneously, I shall be conclusively presumed to have survived that beneficiary for purposes of this will.

☐ I appoint _____, my _____
           [full name of executor]   [relationship]

of _____, as Executor, to serve
           [address of executor]

without bond. If not surviving or otherwise unable to serve, I appoint

_____ , my _____
      [full name of alternate executor]   [relationship]

of _____, as Alternate
           [address of alternate executor]

Executor, also to serve without bond.

In addition to any powers, authority, and discretion granted by law, I grant such Executor or Alternate Executor any and all powers to perform any acts, in his or her sole discretion and without court approval, for the management and distribution of my estate, including independent administration of my estate.

☐ If a Guardian is needed for any of my minor children, I appoint

_____, my _____,
                [name of guardian]   [relationship]

of _____
                          [address of guardian]

as Guardian of the person(s) and property of my minor children, to serve without bond. If not surviving or unable to serve, I appoint

_____, my _____,
          [name of alternate guardian]   [relationship]

of _____
                   [address of alternate guardian]

as alternate Guardian, also to serve without bond.

In addition to any powers, authority, and discretion granted by law, I grant such Guardian or Alternate Guardian any and all powers to perform any acts, in his or her sole discretion and without court approval, for the management and distribution of the property of my minor children.

☐ If any of my children are under _____ on my death, I
                                                      [21, 25, or 30 years old]

direct that any property that I give them under this will be held in an individual trust for each child, under the following terms, until each shall reach

_____.
[21, 25, or 30 years old]

A.   I appoint _____, my _____,
                                   [name of trustee]   [relationship]

of _____,
                          [address of trustee]

as trustee of any and all required trusts, to serve without bond. If not surviving or otherwise unable to serve, then I appoint _____,
                                                                                              [name of

_____, my _____,
              alternate trustee]   [relationship]

of _____,
                   [address of alternate trustee]

as alternate Trustee, also to serve without bond. In addition to all powers, authority, and discretion granted by law, I grant such trustee or alternate trustee full power to perform any act, in his or her sole discretion and without court approval, to distribute and manage the assets of any such trust.

B.   In the trustee's sole discretion, the trustee may distribute any or all of the principal, income, or both as deemed necessary for the beneficiary's health, support, welfare, and education. Any income not distributed shall be added to the trust principal.

C.   Any such trust shall terminate when the beneficiary reaches the required age, when the beneficiary dies prior to reaching the required age, or when all trust funds have been distributed. Upon termination, any remaining undistributed principal and income shall pass to the beneficiary; or if not surviving, to the beneficiary's heirs; or if none, to the residue of my estate.

I publish and sign this Last Will and Testament, consisting of _____ typewritten pages, on _____, 19 _____, and declare that I do so freely, for the purposes expressed, under no constraint or undue influence, and that I am of sound mind and of legal age.

_____
Signature of Testator

_____
Printed name of Testator

On _____, 19 _____, in the presence of all of us, the above-named Testator published and signed this Last Will and Testament, and then at Testator's request, and in Testator's presence, and in each other's presence, we all signed below as witnesses, and we declare, under penalty of perjury, that, to the best of our knowledge, the Testator signed this instrument freely, under no constraint or undue influence, and is of sound mind and legal age.

_____

Signature of Witness

_____

Printed name of Witness

_____

Address of Witness

_____

Signature of Witness

_____

Printed name of Witness

_____

Address of Witness

_____

Signature of Witness

_____

Printed name of Witness

_____

Address of Witness

Chapter 8

Sample Will

In this chapter, a complete sample will is presented. It was prepared using the will clauses contained in Chapter 6. By reviewing this sample will, you will be able to see what a completed will should look like and how the various parts are put together.

The sample will in this chapter is an example of one of the most complex wills which may be prepared using this book. It uses virtually all of the various clauses which may be necessary in a will, whether shown in Chapter 6 as mandatory or optional clauses. Examine the clauses to see how your typewritten final will should look upon completion.

Sample Will

In this sample will, a Mrs. Mary Smith is the fictional testator. Mrs. Smith is married to Mr. John Smith, and they have two minor children who live with them. In her will, Mrs. Smith wishes to accomplish the following:

- ❑ Leave her oval diamond necklace to a friend;
- ❑ Leave her brown mink coat to her mother;
- ❑ Leave $10,000 to each of her children, to be held in trust until they are 21;
- ❑ Leave all the rest of her estate to her husband;
- ❑ Forgive a $1,000.00 debt owed by one of her sisters;

- ❑ Appoint her husband to act as:
     - Executor of the will;
     - Guardian of the children;
     - Trustee of the children's trust;
- ❑ Declare her intention to be an organ donor;
- ❑ Designate her intentions for funeral arrangements.

The following will clauses from Chapter 6 are used by Mrs. Smith to prepare a will which accomplishes all of these purposes:

- ❑ Title Clause
- ❑ Identification Clause
- ❑ Marital Status Clauses
- ❑ Children Identification Clause
- ❑ Entire Estate Gift Clause
- ❑ Specific Gifts Clause
- ❑ Residuary Clause
- ❑ Debt Forgiveness Clause
- ❑ Survivorship Clause
- ❑ Disinheritance Clause
- ❑ Executor Clause
- ❑ Guardianship Clause
- ❑ Children's Trust Fund Clause
- ❑ Organ Donation Clause
- ❑ Funeral Arrangements Clause
- ❑ Signature and Witness Clause
- ❑ Self-Proving Affidavit

By filling in the appropriate blanks in these will clauses, the fictional Mrs. Mary Smith is able to easily and quickly prepare a will which accomplishes all of her desires. She may rest assured that, by having properly prepared and signed a Last Will and Testament, her wishes will be carried out on her death. Please note that when describing the length of this will, it is described as "4 typewritten pages". The Self-Proving Affidavit which is also prepared is not considered an actual part of the will and is not included in the page count. The Self-Proving Affidavit should be prepared on a single sheet of paper separate from the rest of the will. It may, however, be stapled to the will, as explained in the instructions contained in Chapter 9. It would be advisable that Mrs. Smith's husband also prepare a will which includes similar provisions for survivorship and reciprocal provisions for guardianship and trust funds.

Last Will and Testament

of Mary Ellen Smith

I, MARY ELLEN SMITH, a resident of the Town of Centerville, County of Washington and State of Illinois, declare that this is my Last Will and Testament and I revoke all previous Wills and Codicils.

1. I am married to JOHN ALAN SMITH.

2. I was previously married to Robert David Jones. That marriage ended in 1980 by divorce.

3. I have 2 (two) children living. Their names, addresses, and dates of birth are:

    ALICE MARY SMITH,
    16 Main Street,
    Centerville, Illinois
    Born April 21, 1984

    JAMES JOHN SMITH,
    16 Main Street,
    Centerville, Illinois
    Born October 26, 1986

4. I make the following specific gifts:

    I give my Tiffany Oval Diamond and Gold Necklace to my good friend, Susie Mitchell, of Hilltown, Indiana, or, if not surviving, to the residue of my estate.

    I give my Brown Mink Coat, which was a gift from my husband, to my mother, Mrs. Mary Stuart of Naples, Florida, or, if not surviving, to my husband, John Alan Smith.

I give Ten Thousand Dollars, cash, ($10,000.00) to my daughter, Alice Mary Smith, or, if not surviving, to the residue of my estate.

I give Ten Thousand Dollars, cash, ($10,000.00) to my son, James John Smith or, if not surviving, to the residue of my estate.

5.   I give all the rest of my property, whether real or personal, wherever located, to my husband, John Alan Smith, or, if not surviving, to my children, Alice Mary Smith and James John Smith, in equal shares.

6.   I forgive the following debt owed to me: One Thousand Dollars ($1,000.00) due from my sister, Jane Smith, of New York, New York.

7.   All beneficiaries named in this will must survive me by thirty days to receive any gift under this will. If any beneficiary and I should die simultaneously, I shall be conclusively presumed to have survived that beneficiary for purposes of this will.

8.   I intentionally disinherit anyone not specifically named as a beneficiary in this will.

9.   I appoint my husband, John Alan Smith, as Executor, to serve without bond. If not surviving or otherwise unable to serve, I appoint my brother, Harold Stuart, of Chicago, Illinois, as alternate Executor, also to serve without bond. In addition to any powers, authority, and discretion granted by law, I grant my Executor or my alternate Executor full power to perform any acts, in his or her sole discretion and without court approval, for the management and distribution of my estate, including independent administration of my estate.

10.   If a Guardian is needed for any of my minor children, I appoint my husband, John Alan Smith, as Guardian of the person(s) and property of my minor children, to serve without bond. If not surviving or otherwise unable to serve, I appoint my sister, Sally Stuart Hall, of Des Moines, Iowa, as alternate Guardian, also to serve without bond. In addition to any powers, authority, and discretion granted by law, I grant such Guardian or alternate Guardian full power to perform any acts, in his or her sole discretion and without court approval, for the management and distribution of the property of my minor children.

11.   If any of my children are under the age of 21 on my death, I direct that any property that I give them under this will be held in an individual trust for each child, under the following terms, until each shall reach 21 years of age.

A.   I appoint, my husband, John Alan Smith, as trustee of any and all required trusts, to serve without bond. If not surviving or otherwise unable to serve, then I appoint my sister, Sally Stuart Hall, as alternate Trustee, also to serve without bond. In addition to all powers, authority, and discretion granted by law, I grant the trustee or alternate trustee full power to perform any act, in his or her sole discretion and without court approval, to distribute and manage the assets of any such trust.

B.   In the trustee's sole discretion, the trustee may distribute any or all of the principal, income, or both as deemed necessary for the beneficiary's health, support, welfare, and education. Any income not distributed shall be added to the trust principal.

C.   Any such trust shall terminate when the beneficiary reaches the required age, when the beneficiary dies prior to reaching the required age, or when all trust funds have been distributed. Upon termination, remaining undistributed principal and income shall pass to the beneficiary; or if not surviving, to the beneficiary's heirs; or if none, to the residue of my estate.

12.   I declare that, pursuant to the Uniform Anatomical Gift Act, I wish to donate any of my body parts and/or organs to any medical institution willing to accept them, and I direct my Executor to carry out such donation.

13.   I have made funeral arrangements with Centerville Funeral Parlor, Centerville, Illinois for burial at Shady Hill Cemetery, Centerville, Illinois, and I direct my Executor to carry out such arrangements.

I publish and sign this Last Will and Testament, consisting of 4 (four) typewritten pages, on January 1, 1992, and declare that I do so freely, for the purposes expressed, under no constraint or undue influence, and that I am of sound mind and of legal age.

Mary Ellen Smith
Mary Ellen Smith

On January 1, 1992, in the presence of all of us, the above-named Testator published and signed this Last Will and Testament, and then, at Testator's request, and in Testator's presence, and in each other's presence, we all signed below as witnesses, and we declare, under penalty of perjury, that, to the best of our knowledge, the Testator signed this instrument freely, under no constraint or undue influence, and is of sound mind and legal age.

Joan Andrews, of Centerville, Illinois
Joan Andrews

Christopher Williams, of Centerville, Illinois
Christopher Williams

Sandra Wright, of Centerville, Illinois
Sandra Wright

Self-Proving Affidavit

We, the undersigned Testator and witnesses, being first sworn on oath and under penalty of perjury, state that in the presence of all the witnesses, the Testator published and signed the above Last Will and Testament and then, at Testator's request and in the presence of the Testator, and in each other's presence, each of the witnesses signed as witnesses, and that, to the best of our knowledge, the Testator signed said Last Will and Testament freely, under no constraint or undue influence, and is of sound mind and legal age.

Mary Ellen Smith, Testator, of Centerville, Illinois
Mary Ellen Smith

Joan Andrews, witness, of Centerville, Illinois
Joan Andrews

Christopher Williams, witness, of Centerville, Illinois
Christopher Williams

Sandra Wright, witness, of Centerville, Illinois
Sandra Wright

County of Washington   } SS.
State of Illinois   }

Subscribed, sworn to, and acknowledged before me on January 1, 1992, by MARY ELLEN SMITH, the testator, and JOAN ANDREWS, CHRISTOPHER WILLIAMS, and SANDRA WRIGHT, the witnesses.

Robert Merlin   Notary Public,
Robert Merlin   In and for the County of Washington,
                  State of Illinois

Chapter 9

Preparing Your Will

As you have noted in the sample will in the previous chapter, there is nothing very complicated about the arrangement of your will. This chapter will explain how to put your own will together and properly type or have it typed and readied for your signature. Using your Property and Beneficiary Questionnaires as a guide, you should already have selected and filled in the appropriate information on either your individual will clauses from those contained in Chapter 6 or chosen and filled in the necessary information on one of the pre-assembled wills from Chapter 7.

Below are instructions for preparing the final version of your will. As you go about preparing your will, take your time and be very careful to proofread the original before you sign it to be certain that it exactly states your desires. [Note: At the end of this chapter are detailed instructions to be followed for preparing your will if you are a resident of the State of Louisiana.]

Instructions for Preparing Your Will

1.   Chapter 6 Will: If you are preparing a will from separate clauses in Chapter 6, you should have a photo-copy worksheet version of all of the clauses that you have selected and already filled-in for your own will. Don't forget to include all of those clauses which are indicated as "Mandatory".

Chapter 7 Will: If you are preparing a will from a pre-assembled will, you should have before you a completed and filled-in photo-copy worksheet of the pre-assembled will which you have chosen.

For all wills: You should also have before you a photo-copy worksheet version of a filled-in Self-Proving Affidavit from Chapter 6.

2.   On the photo-copy worksheet version of your will, cross out all of the instructions and any other extraneous material which is not to become a part of your will. In consecutive order, number each clause of your will in the boxes provided for that purpose at the beginning of each clause. Begin your numbering of clauses with the clause defining your marital status. End your numbering of clauses with the clause directly before the paragraph which begins: "**I publish and sign this Last Will and Testament, consisting of** . . ."

3.   When you have completed numbering your will clauses, carefully re-read the entire worksheet version of your will to be certain that it is exactly as you wish.

4.   After making any necessary changes, type or have typed the entire will on good quality 8 1/2 X 11" typing paper. Type the "Self-Proving Affidavit" on a separate sheet of paper, as it is technically not a part of your will, but rather a separate and distinct document.

5.   After you have completed typing your will, fill in the total number of pages in the Signature paragraph. Do not yet sign your will or affidavit or fill in the date in any of the spaces indicated.

6.   Again, very carefully proofread your entire will. Be certain that there are no errors. If there are any errors, re-type that particular page. ***Do not*** attempt to correct any errors with white-out type correcting fluid or with erasures of any kind. ***Do not*** cross-out or add anything to the typewritten words using a pen or pencil. Your will, when completed properly, should look similar to the sample will contained in the previous chapter, except that the signature and date spaces should be blank.

7.   When you have a perfect original of your will, with no corrections and no additions, staple all of the pages together in the top left hand corner. The Self-Proving Affidavit should be stapled together at the end of your will also. You are now ready to prepare for the *execution* (signing) of your will. Please turn to the Chapter 10 for instruction on signing your will.

Special Instructions For Residents of Louisiana

If you are a resident of Louisiana, the laws which govern your state are somewhat different than those of the other 49 states. The reason for this is that Louisiana law is derived from the French Civil Code rather than the English Common Law or Spanish Law as are all of the other states.

Essentially, it is only the format of your will which is changed for use in Louisiana. Please carefully follow the instructions below for the preparation of your will for Louisiana. As you are preparing your will following the instructions in this chapter, you should make the following changes:

1.   After the title of your will (LAST WILL AND TESTAMENT OF *[your name]*) and before the first paragraph of your will, correctly fill in the blanks and insert the following paragraph:

Before me, _____, Clerk of
                              [name of District Court Clerk]
the _____ District Court in and for the Parish of
          [name of Court]
_____, being duly commissioned and
          [name of parish]
qualified as such, and ex officio Notary Public, in the presence of 3 (three) competent witnesses residing in the Parish of _____,
                                                                  [parish where witnesses reside]
State of Louisiana, _____, a resident of
                              [name of testator]
_____,
     [name of city or Parish where testator resides]
State of Louisiana, personally came before me, the Notary, and declared to me, the Notary, in the presence of the undersigned witnesses that _____
                                                                                          [she or he]
wished to make _____ Last Will and Testament and that _____
                    [her or his]   *[she or he]*
wished that I, the Notary, receive _____ Last Will and Testament;
                                          [her or his]
and _____ then dictated to me the following Last Will and Testament
     [she or he]
in the presence of the 3 (three) witnesses; and I, the Notary, received it from said dictation and wrote it down exactly as it was dictated to me in the presence of the testator and the 3 (three) witnesses, in the following words, to wit:

2.   At this point, as you are assembling your will, you should insert your entire will as prepared using Chapters 6 or 7, except do not use anything after the paragraph which begins: "I publish and sign this Last Will and Testament, consisting of ...".

Instead, fill in the correct insertions below and use the following at the end of your will:

This Last Will and Testament of _____ was dictated by
                                                    [your name]
the testator to me, the Notary, in the presence and hearing of the 3 (three) witnesses and was reduced to writing by me, the Notary, as dictated. I, the Notary, then read the above Last Will and Testament to the testator in the presence of the 3 (three) witnesses, and the testator, being satisfied with said Last Will and Testament then signed it in my presence and in the presence of the 3 (three) witnesses, and this all having been done, received, dictated, read, and signed at one time, without any interruption, and without turning aside to do any other act, in the Parish of_____, State of
                                                    [name of parish]
Louisiana, on _____, 19__.
                        [date]

_____
Signature of Testator

_____
Printed name of Testator

_____
Signature of Notary Public

_____
Printed name of Notary Public

Notary Public,
In and for the Parish of _____,
State of Louisiana.

On _____, 19 _____, in the presence of all of us, the
[date]
above-named testator signed and declared to us that this is _____ Last
[her or his]
Will and Testament, and then at testator's request, and in _____
[her or his]
presence, and in each other's presence, we all signed below as witnesses,
and we declare, under penalty of perjury, that, to the best of our knowledge,
the testator signed this instrument freely, under no constraint or undue
influence, and is of sound mind and legal age.

_____
Signature of Witness

_____
Printed name of Witness

_____
Address of Witness

_____
Signature of Witness

_____
Printed name of Witness

_____
Address of Witness

_____
Signature of Witness

_____
Printed name of Witness

_____
Address of Witness

3.   When you have assembled your entire will and had it typewritten as indicated earlier in this chapter for all wills, you must go with your 3 (three) witnesses and take your Louisiana will to the Clerk of the District Court for the Parish in which you reside. Request that the Clerk/Notary Public transcribe your will exactly as you dictate it to him or her.

4.   After you have dictated your will to the Clerk and he or she has written it out, you, the Notary Public, and the 3 (three) witnesses must sign the will where indicated. You need not use the "Self-Proving Affidavit" shown at the end of Chapter 6 and you need not follow the steps outlined in Chapter 10 as they pertain to signing your will. Once completed as outlined above, the written version of your Last Will and Testament is valid as a will in the State of Louisiana.

Chapter 10

Signing Your Will

After you have successfully had your will typed in the proper form, you are ready to sign it. **Do not** sign your will until you have read this chapter and have all of the necessary witnesses and Notary Public present. The legal requirements of this chapter regarding the proper execution (signing) of your will are extremely important and must not be deviated from in any manner for your will to be legally valid. These requirements are not at all difficult to follow, but they must be followed precisely. It is these formal requirements that transform your will from a mere piece of paper outlining your wishes to a legal document which grants the power to dispose of your property under court order after your death.

The reasons for the formality of these requirements are two-fold: first, by requiring a ceremonial-type signing of the document, it is hoped that the testator is made fully aware of the importance of what he or she is doing; and second, by requiring a formal signing witnessed by other adults, it is hoped that any instances of forgery, fraud, and coercion will be avoided, or at least minimized.

Again, these legal formalities must be observed strictly. **Do not** deviate from these instructions in any way. It is the formal execution or signing of your will that makes it legally valid and failure to properly sign your will will render it invalid. To properly execute your will, follow these few simple steps:

Instructions for Signing Your Will:

1. Select 3 (three) witnesses who will be available to assist you in witnessing your will. These persons may be any adults who are not mentioned in the will either as a beneficiary, executor, trustee, or guardian. They may be friends, neighbors, co-workers, even strangers. However, it is prudent to choose persons who have been stable members of your community, since they may be called upon to testify in court someday.

2. Arrange for all of your witnesses to meet you at the office or home of a local Notary Public. Many banks, real estate offices, and government offices have notary services and most will be glad to assist you. (The Notary Public may *not* be one of the required three witnesses.)

3. In front of all of the witnesses and in front of the Notary Public, the following should take place in the order shown:

    ❑   You should state: "This is my Last Will and Testament, which I am about to sign. I ask that each of you witness my signature." There is no requirement that the witnesses know any of the terms of your will or that they read any of your will. All that is necessary is that they hear you state that it is your will, that you request them to be witnesses, that they observe you sign your will, and that they also sign the will as witnesses in each other's presence.

    ❑   You will then sign your will at the end, exactly as your name is typewritten on your will, in the two (2) places indicated, in ink using a pen. Don't forget that one of your signatures will be on the "Self-Proving Affidavit".

    ❑   After you have signed, pass your will to the first witness, who should sign in the two (2) places indicated and fill in his or her address. Don't forget that one of the two places that each witness will sign is on the "Self-Proving Affidavit".

    ❑   After the first witness has signed, have the will passed to the second Witness, who should also sign in the two (2) places indicated and fill in his or her address.

    ❑   After the second witness has signed, have the will passed to the third and final witness, who also signs in the two (2) places indicated and fills in his or her address. Throughout this ceremony, you and all of the witnesses must remain together. It is easier if you are all seated around a table or desk.

❑   The final step is for the Notary Public to sign in the space indicated. When this step is completed, your will is a valid legal document and you may be assured that your wishes will be carried out upon its presentation to a probate court on your death.

Please note that you should *never* under any circumstances sign a duplicate of your will. Once it has been properly executed following the steps above, you may make photocopies of your will. It is a good idea to label any of these as "COPIES".

Safeguarding Your Will

Having completed your will according to the foregoing instructions, it is now time to place your will in a safe place. Many people keep their important papers in a safety deposit box at a local bank. Although this is an acceptable place for storing a will, be advised that there are certain drawbacks. Your will should be in a place which is readily accessible to your executor at a moment's notice. Often there are certain unavoidable delays in gaining access to a safety deposit box in an emergency situation. If you are married, and your safety deposit box is jointly held, many of these delays can be avoided. However, even in this situation, some states prevent immediate access to the safety deposit box of a deceased married person. If you decide to keep the original in your safe deposit box, it is a good idea to keep a clearly marked copy of your will at home in a safe but easily located place, with a note as to where the original may be found.

An acceptable alternative to a safety deposit box is a home file box or desk that is used for home storage of your important papers. If possible, this storage place should be fireproof and under lock and key. Wherever you decide to store your will, you will need to inform your chosen executor of its location. The executor will need to obtain the original of your will shortly after your demise to determine if there are any necessary duties which must be looked after without delay, for example: funeral plans or organ donations.

It is also a good practice to store any life insurance policies and a copy of your birth certificate in the same location. Additionally, it is also prudent to store a copy of your Property Questionnaire, your Beneficiary Questionnaire, and the Executor Information List with your will in order to provide your executor with an inventory and location list of your assets and a list of information regarding your heirs and beneficiaries. Any title documents or deeds relating to property which will be transferred under your will may also be stored with your will for the convenience of your executor. A final precaution is, if you desire, to allow the executor whom you have named to keep a copy of your will. Be careful, however, to be certain that you immediately inform him or her of any new wills which you prepare or of any *codicils* to your will (formal changes to your will) or of any decision to revoke your will.

Chapter 11

Changing Your Will

In this chapter, instructions will be given on when and how to change your will and how to revoke your will. It is most important to follow these instructions carefully should you desire to make *any* changes to your will. Failure to follow these instructions and an attempt to change your will by such methods as crossing out a name or penciling in an addition could have the disastrous effect of voiding portions of or, perhaps, even your entire will. Again, these instructions are not difficult to follow, but are very important to insure that your will remains legally valid.

If you desire to totally revoke your will, there are two acceptable methods:

❑   By signing a new will which expressly states that you revoke all prior wills. All wills prepared using this book contain such a provision.

❑   By completely destroying, burning, or mutilating your will, while it is in your possession if you actually intend that there be a revocation of your will.

Regarding any potential changes which you may wish to make in your will at a later date, you should periodically review the provisions of your will, keeping in mind the following items as they relate to your present situation:

❑   Have there been any substantial changes in your personal wealth?

❑   Have there been any changes in your ownership of any property mentioned in your will?

❑   Have any of the beneficiaries named in your will died or fallen into your disfavor?

❑   Are any of the persons whom you named as executor, guardian, or trustee in your will no longer willing or able to serve?

❑   Have you changed the state of your residence?

❑   Have you been married since the date of your will?

❑   Have you been divorced since the date of your will?

❑   Have you had any children since the date of your will?

❑   Have you adopted any children since the date of your will?

❑   Do you simply wish to make any corrections, deletions, or additions to any provisions in your will?

If any of these matters apply, you will need to change your will accordingly. Although it is possible to completely re-write your will to take account of any of these changes, an easier method is to prepare and formally execute a *codicil*, or a written change to a will. Please bear in mind that all of the formalities surrounding the signing of your original will must again be followed for any such changes contained in a codicil to your will to be valid.

Never attempt to change any portions of your will by any other method. For example, ***do not*** attempt to add provisions in the margin of your will, either by typing them in or by writing them in. ***Do not*** attempt to cross-out any portions of your will. These methods are not acceptable methods for the alteration of a will, and could subject your will to a court battle to determine its subsequent validity.

The following is a general form for a codicil and standard clauses for changing provisions of your will. Insert such changes as are necessary where indicated on the form and number each clause accordingly. Prepare it as you prepared your original will using the following simple list of instructions:

Instructions for Preparing Your Codicil

1. Read through the codicil clauses on the following pages. Make a photo-copy of all of the codicil clauses that you select for use in your codicil. Using the photo-copies as a worksheet, fill in the appropriate information on each chosen clause. Don't forget to include all of those clauses which are indicated as "Mandatory".

2. On your photo-copy worksheet version, cross out all of the instructions and any other extraneous material which are not to become a part of your codicil. In consecutive order, number each clause of your codicil in the boxes provided for that purpose at the beginning of each clause. End your numbering of clauses with the clause directly before the paragraph which begins: "I republish my Last Will and Testament ..."

3. When you have completed numbering your codicil clauses, carefully re-read your entire codicil to be certain that it is exactly as you wish.

4. After making any necessary changes, type or have typed the entire codicil on good quality 8 1/2 X 11" typing paper. Type the "Self-Proving Affidavit" on a separate sheet of paper, as it is technically not a part of your codicil, but rather a separate and distinct document.

5. After you have completed typing your codicil, fill in the total number of pages in the Signature paragraph. Do not yet sign your codicil or fill in the date in any of the spaces indicated.

6. Again, very carefully proofread your entire codicil. Be certain that there are no errors. If there are any errors, re-type that particular page. *Do not* attempt to correct any errors with white-out type correcting fluid or with erasures of any kind. *Do not* cross-out or add anything to the typewritten words using a pen or pencil.

7. When you have a perfect original of your codicil, with no corrections and no additions, staple all of the pages together in the top left hand corner. The Self-Proving Affidavit should be stapled together at the end of your codicil also. You are now ready to prepare for the *execution* (signing) of your codicil. For signing your codicil, please follow the same instructions that are provided in Chapter 10 for signing your will, substituting the statement "This is my Codicil to my Last Will and Testament that I am about to sign".

Codicil Clauses

Title

Mandatory: The below title is mandatory for all codicils and must be included. Fill in the name blank with your full legal name. If you have been known under more than one name, use your principal name. Be sure to use the exact same name as you used in the will that you are changing. Do not number this title.

CODICIL TO THE LAST WILL AND TESTAMENT OF _____
[your full name]

Identification Clause

Mandatory. This clause must be included in all codicils. Do not number this clause. In the first blank, include any other names which you are known by. Do this by adding the phrase: "also known as" after your principal full name. For example: *John James Smith, also known as Jimmy John Smith.* Be sure to use the exact same name as you used in the will that you are changing. In the spaces provided for your residence, use the location of your principal residence: where you currently live permanently.

I, _____, a resident
[your full name and any other names that you have used]
of _____, _____,
[name of city or town]   *[name of county]*
_____, make this Codicil to my Last Will and
[name of state]
Testament dated _____, 19 _____.
[date]

Addition to Will Clause

Optional: Use this clause if you wish to add additional provisions to your will. In the space provided, simply fill in whatever provisions you desire to be added.

> ☐ I add the following sentence to Clause # _____ of my will:

Revocation of Paragraph of Will Clause

Optional: This clause should be used in those situations in which you desire to delete a clause from your original will. Simply indicate which clause that you desire to revoke in the space indicated.

> ☐ I revoke Clause # _____ of my will.

Correction of Will Clause

Optional: This clause is used in those situations in which you wish to retain a particular clause in your will, but desire to change a portion of it (for example: substitution of the name of a different beneficiary). Where indicated in this clause, type the correct information that you wish to have become part of your will.

> ☐ I change Clause # _____ of my will to read as follows:

Signature and Witness Clauses

Mandatory: All of the following remaining portions of your codicil are mandatory and must be included in your codicil. Do not number any of these provisions. You will fill in the number of pages and the appropriate dates where indicated after you have properly typed or had your codicil typed.

I republish my Last Will and Testament, dated _____, 19 _____, as modified by this Codicil. I have signed this Codicil to my Will, consisting of _____ typewritten pages, on _____, 19 _____, and declare that I do so freely, for the purposes expressed, under no constraint or undue influence, and that I am of sound mind and of legal age.

_____
Signature of Testator

_____
Printed name of Testator

On _____, 19 _____, in the presence of all of us, the above-named Testator published and signed this Codicil, and then at Testator's request, and in Testator's presence, and in each other's presence, we all signed below as witnesses, and we declare, under penalty of perjury, that, to the best of our knowledge, the Testator signed this instrument freely, under no constraint or undue influence, and is of sound mind and legal age.

_____
Signature of Witness

_____
Printed name of Witness

_____
Address of Witness

Signature of Witness

Printed name of Witness

Address of Witness

Signature of Witness

Printed name of Witness

Address of Witness

Codicil Self-Proving Affidavit

Although use of this clause is not a strict legal necessity, it is strongly recommended that you prepare and use this Affidavit with all codicils. Although a few states have not enacted legislation to allow for their use in court, the current trend is for all courts to allow their use. This Affidavit will allow for your signature on your codicil to be proved without the necessity of having the three witnesses appear in court, a point which will save time, money, and trouble in having your codicil admitted to probate when necessary.

SELF-PROVING AFFIDAVIT

We, the undersigned Testator and witnesses, being first sworn on oath and under penalty of perjury, state that, in the presence of all the witnesses, the Testator published and signed the above Codicil to _____ Last Will
[her or his]
and Testament and then, at Testator's request, and in the presence of the Testator and of each other, each of the witnesses signed as witnesses, and that, to the best of our knowledge, the Testator signed said Codicil freely, under no constraint or undue influence, and is of sound mind and legal age.

_____
Signature of Testator

_____
Printed name of Testator

_____
Signature of Witness

_____
Printed name of Witness

_____
Address of Witness

_____
Signature of Witness

_____
Printed name of Witness

_____
Address of Witness

_____
Signature of Witness

_____
Printed name of Witness

_____
Address of Witness

County of _____}   SS.
State of _____}

Subscribed, sworn to, and acknowledged before me on _____,
19_____ by _____, the testator, and
                          [full name of testator]

by _____,
              [full name of first witness]

_____,
              [full name of second witness]

_____,
              [full name of third witness]
the Witnesses.

_____
Signature of Notary Public

_____
Printed name of Notary Public

Notary Public,
In and for the County of _____,
State of _____.

Chapter 12

Preparing a Living Will

In this chapter, you will be given instructions on how to prepare a living will. A living will is a relatively new legal document which has been made necessary by the advent of recent technological advances in the field of medicine which can allow for the continued existence of a person on advanced "life support" systems long after any normal semblance of "life", as many people consider it, has ceased.

The inherent problem which is raised by this type of extraordinary medical "life support" is that the person whose life is being artificially continued by such means may not wish to be kept alive beyond what they may consider to be the proper time for their life to end. However, since a person in such condition has no method of communicating their wishes to the medical or legal authorities in charge, a living will was developed which allows one to make these important decisions in advance of the situation.

As more and more advances are made in the medical field in terms of the ability to prevent "clinical" death, the difficult situations envisioned by a living will are destined to occur more often. The legal acceptance of a living will is currently at the forefront of new laws being added in many states.

Although this living will does not address all possible contingencies regarding terminally ill patients, it does provide a written declaration for the individual to make known his or her decisions on life-prolonging procedures.

A living will declares your wishes not to be kept alive by artificial or mechanical means if you are suffering from a terminal condition and your death would be imminent without the use of such artificial means. It provides a legally-binding written set of instructions regarding your wishes about this important matter.

In order to qualify for the use of a living will, you must meet the following criteria:

❑   You must be at least 19 years of age;

❑   You must be of "sound mind" and able to comprehend the nature of your action in signing such a document.

If you desire that your life not be prolonged artificially when there is no reasonable chance for recovery and death is imminent, please follow the instructions below for completion of your living will. The entire following form is mandatory. It has been adapted to be valid in all states which currently recognize living wills. Even in those states that have not yet enacted legislation providing express statutory recognition of living wills, courts, health care professionals, and physicians will be guided by this expression of your desires concerning life support. Please consult the Appendix for further information regarding recognition of living wills in your state.

Instructions for Preparing and Signing a Living Will

1.   Make a photo-copy of the entire living will form from this chapter. Using the photo-copy as a worksheet, please fill in the correct information in the appropriate blanks.

2.   On clean, white, 8 1/2 X 11" paper, have typed or type yourself the entire living will exactly as shown with your information added. Carefully re-read this original living will to be certain that it exactly expresses your desires on this very important matter. When you have a clean, clear original typed version, staple all of the pages together in the upper left-hand corner. *Do not* yet sign this document or fill in the date.

3.   You should now assemble three witnesses and a Notary Public to witness your signature. As noted on the document itself, these witnesses should have no connection with you from a health care or beneficiary standpoint. Specifically, the beneficiaries must:

❑   Be at least 19 years of age.

❑   Not be related to you in any manner: by blood, marriage, or adoption.

❑   Not be your attending physician, or a patient or employee of your attending physician; or a patient, physician, or employee of the health care facility in which you may be a patient. However, please see below.

❑   Not be entitled to any portion of your estate on your death under any laws of intestate succession, nor under your will or any codicil.

❑   Have no claim against any portion of your estate on your death.

❑   Not be directly financially responsible for your medical care.

❑   Not have signed the living will for you, even at your direction.

❑   Not be paid a fee for acting as a witness.

❑   In addition, please note that 12 states and the District of Columbia have laws in effect regarding witnesses when the declarant is a patient in a nursing home, boarding facility, hospital, or skilled or intermediate health care facility. In those situation, it is advisable to have a patient ombudsman, patient advocate, or the director of the health care facility to act as the third witness to the signing of a living will. These states are: California, Delaware, District of Columbia, Georgia, Massachusetts, Michigan, Nebraska, New Hampshire, New Jersey, Ohio, Pennsylvania, Rhode Island, and South Dakota.

4.   In front of all of the witnesses and in front of the Notary Public, the following should take place in the order shown:

❑   You should state: "This is my living will which I am about to sign. I ask that each of you witness my signature." There is no requirement that the witnesses know any of the terms of your living will or that they read any of your living will. All that is necessary is that they hear you state that it is your living will, that you request them to be witnesses, that they observe you sign your living will and that they also sign the living will as witnesses in each other's presence.

❑   You will then sign your living will at the end, exactly as your name is typewritten on your living will, where indicated, in ink using a pen.

❑   After you have signed, pass your living will to the first witness, who should sign where indicated and fill in his or her address.

❑ After the first witness has signed, have the living will passed to the second witness, who should also sign where indicated.

❑ After the second witness has signed, have the living will passed to the third and final witness, who also signs where indicated and fills in his or her address. Throughout this ceremony, you and all of the witnesses must remain together.

❑ The final step is for the Notary Public to sign in the space indicated. When this step is completed, your living will is a valid legal document. Have several copies made and, if appropriate, deliver a copy to your attending physician to have placed in your medical records file. You may also desire to give a copy to the person you have chosen as the executor of your will, a copy to your clergy, and a copy to your spouse or other trusted relative.

❑ California and Georgia require that you periodically re-sign your living will for it to remain valid. For California, simply re-sign and re-date your original living will within 5 years of the original date of signing and for Georgia, re-sign it within 7 years.

Living Will Declaration and Directive to Physicians

of _____
[your full name]

I, _____, willfully and voluntarily make known my
[your full name]
desire that my life not be artificially prolonged under the circumstances set forth below, and, pursuant to any and all applicable laws in the State of
_____ I declare that:
[name of state]

1. If at any time I should have an incurable injury, disease, or illness which has been certified as a terminal condition by my attending physician and one additional physician, both of whom have personally examined me, and such physicians have determined that there can be no recovery from such condition and my death is imminent, and where the application of life prolonging procedures would serve only to artificially prolong the dying process, I direct that such procedures be withheld or withdrawn, and that I be permitted to die naturally with only the administration of medication, the administration of nutrition, or the performance of any medical procedure deemed necessary to provide me with comfort, care, or to alleviate pain.

2. If at any time I should have been diagnosed as being in a persistent vegetative state which has been certified as incurable by my attending physician and one additional physician, both of whom have personally examined me, and such physicians have determined that there can be no recovery from such condition, and where the application of life prolonging procedures would serve only to artificially prolong the dying process, I direct that such procedures be withheld or withdrawn, and that I be permitted to die naturally with only the administration of medication, the administration of nutrition, or the performance of any medical procedure deemed necessary to provide me with comfort, care, or to alleviate pain.

3. In the absence of my ability to give directions regarding my treatment in the above situations, including directions regarding the use of such life prolonging procedures, it is my intention that this declaration shall be honored by my family, my physician, and any court of law, as the final expression of my legal right to refuse medical and surgical treatment. I declare that I fully accept the consequences for such refusal.

4. If I am diagnosed as pregnant, this document shall have no force and effect during my pregnancy.

5. I understand the full importance of this declaration, and I am emotionally and mentally competent to make this declaration and Living Will. No person shall be in any way responsible for the making or placing into effect of this declaration and Living Will or for carrying out my express directions. I also understand that I may revoke this document at any time.

I publish and sign this Living Will and Directive to Physicians, consisting of _____ typewritten pages, on _____, 19 _____, and declare that I do so freely, for the purposes expressed, under no constraint or undue influence, and that I am of sound mind and of legal age.

_____
Declarant's Signature

_____
Printed Name of Declarant

On _____, 19 _____, in the presence of all of us, the above-named Declarant published and signed this Living Will and Directive to Physicians, and then at the Declarant's request, and in the Declarant's presence, and in each other's presence, we all signed below as witnesses, and we each declare, under penalty of perjury, that, to the best of our knowledge,

1. The Declarant is personally known to me and, to the best of my knowledge, the Declarant signed this instrument freely, under no constraint or undue influence, and is of sound mind and memory and legal age, and fully aware of the possible consequences of this action.

2. I am at least 19 years of age and I am not related to the Declarant in any manner: by blood, marriage, or adoption.

3. I am not the Declarant's attending physician, or a patient or employee of the Declarant's attending physician; or a patient, physician, or employee of the health care facility in which the Declarant is a patient, unless such person is required or allowed to witness the execution of this document by the laws of the state in which this document is executed.

4. I am not entitled to any portion of the Declarant's estate on the Declarant's death under the laws of intestate succession of any state or country, nor under the Last Will and Testament of the Declarant or any Codicil to such Last Will and Testament.

5. I have no claim against any portion of the Declarant's estate on the Declarant's death.

6. I am not directly financially responsible for the Declarant's medical care.

7. I did not sign the Declarant's signature for the Declarant or on the direction of the Declarant, nor have I been paid any fee for acting as a witness to the execution of this document.

_____
Signature of Witness

_____
Printed name of Witness

_____
Address of Witness

_____
Signature of Witness

_____
Printed name of Witness

_____
Address of Witness

_____

Signature of Witness

_____

Printed name of Witness

_____

Address of Witness

County of _____}   SS.
State of _____}

On _____, 19 _____, before me personally
appeared _____, the Declarant,
          [full name of Declarant]
_____, the first witness,
          [full name of first witness]
_____, the second witness,
          [full name of second witness]
_____, the third witness,
          [full name of third witness]
and, being first sworn on oath and under penalty of perjury, state that, in the
presence of all the witnesses, the Declarant published and signed the above
Living Will Declaration and Directive to Physicians, and then, at Declarant's
request, and in the presence of the Declarant and of each other, each of the
witnesses signed as witnesses, and stated that, to the best of their
knowledge, the Declarant signed said Living Will Declaration and Directive to
Physicians freely, under no constraint or undue influence, and is of sound
mind and memory and legal age and fully aware of the potential
consequences of this action. The witnesses further state that this affidavit is
made at the direction of and in the presence of the Declarant.

_____

Signature of Notary Public

_____

Printed name of Notary Public

Notary Public,
In and for the County of _____,
State of _____.

Revoking Your Living Will

All states which have recognized living wills have provided methods for the easy revocation of them. Since they provide authority for medical personnel to withhold life-support technology which will likely result in death to the patient, great care must be taken to insure that a change of mind by the patient is heeded.

If revocation of your living will is an important issue, please consult your state's law directly. The name of your particular state's law relating to living wills is provided in the Appendix of this book.

For the revocation of a living will, any one of the following methods of revocation is generally acceptable:

❑ Physical destruction of the living will, such as tearing, burning, or mutilating the document.

❑ A written revocation of the living will by you or by a person acting at your direction. A form for this is provided at the end of this chapter. You may use two witnesses on this form, although most states do not require the use of witnesses for the written revocation of a living will to be valid.

❑ An oral revocation in the presence of a witness who signs and dates a writing confirming a revocation. This oral declaration may take any manner. Most states allow for a person to revoke such a document by any indication (even non-verbal) of the intent to revoke a living will, regardless of their physical or mental condition.

To use the Revocation of Living Will form provided on the next page, simply fill in the appropriate information, retype the form, and sign it. In addition, your two witnesses may sign it at the same time.

Revocation of Living Will

I , _____ , am the Declarant
            [your full name]

and maker of a Living Will and Directive to Physicians, dated _____
                                                                [date of
_____ , 19, _____ .
  original Living Will]

By this written revocation, I hereby entirely revoke such Living Will and
Directive to Physicians and intend that it no longer have any force or effect.

Dated _____ , 19 _____ .

_____
Declarant's Signature

_____
Printed Name of Declarant

_____
Signature of Witness

_____
Printed name of Witness

_____
Address of Witness

_____
Signature of Witness

_____
Printed name of Witness

_____
Address of Witness

Chapter 13

Preparing a Durable Power of Attorney

A *power of attorney* form is a document which is used to allow one person to give authority to another person to act on their behalf. The person signing the power of attorney grants legal authority to another to "stand in their shoes" and act legally for them. The person who receives the power of attorney is called an *attorney-in-fact*. This title and the power of attorney form does not mean that the person receiving the power has to be a lawyer.

Power of attorney forms are useful documents for many occasions. They can be used to authorize someone else to sign certain documents if you can not be present when the signatures are necessary. Traditionally, property matters were the type of actions handled with powers of attorney. Increasingly, however, people are using a specific type of power of attorney to authorize other persons to act on their behalf in the event of disability. This broad type of power of attorney is called a *durable* power of attorney. A *durable* power of attorney is intended to remain in effect even if a person becomes disabled or incompetent. All states have passed legislation that specifically authorizes this type of power of attorney. However, a few states require that specific language or forms be used for durable powers of attorney. (Residents of California, Florida, Missouri, Nevada, New York, North Carolina, Oklahoma, Rhode Island, and South Carolina need to consult with the specific laws in their states to determine any procedures or forms required for durable powers of attorney).

The types of powers of attorney included in this chapter and instructions for their use are as follows:

Durable Unlimited Power of Attorney: This form should be used only in the situation in which you desire to authorize another person to act for you in all transactions. The grant of power under this document is unlimited. However, unlike a traditional unlimited power of attorney, this form remains in effect even if you are incapacitated or disabled. This form also allows your attorney-in-fact to act on your behalf in making medical decisions regarding your care. Please be advised that some states may require that you specifically spell out the authority granted to perform certain acts. Generally, however, for personal and property transactions this broad grant of power will be effective to allow your attorney-in-fact to perform on your behalf in the event of your disability. To complete this form the names and addresses of the person granting the power and of the person receiving the power should be filled in. Both persons should sign the document. The signature of the person granting the power should be notarized.

Durable Limited Power of Attorney: This document provides for a limited grant of authority to another person. It should be used if you only need to authorize another to act for you in a specific manner or to perform a specific action. However, this form remains in effect even if you are incapacitated or disabled. This form also allows your attorney-in-fact to act on your behalf in making medical decisions regarding your care. Please be advised that some states may require that you specifically spell out the authority granted to perform certain acts. Generally, however, for personal and property transactions the limited grant of power provided by this document will be effective to allow your attorney-in-fact to perform on your behalf in the event of your disability. To complete this form the names and addresses of the person granting the power and of the person receiving the power should be filled in. A full and detailed description of the powers granted should be inserted. Both persons should sign the document. The signature of the person granting the power should be notarized.

Revocation of Power of Attorney: This document may be used with either of the above two power of attorney forms. It is used to terminate the authority that was granted to the other person in the first place. If the grant of power was for a limited purpose, and that purpose is complete, this revocation should be used as soon after the transaction as possible. In any event, if you choose to revoke a power of attorney, a copy of this revocation should be provided to the person to whom the power was given. Copies should also be given to any party that may have had dealings with the attorney-in-fact before the revocation and to any party with whom the attorney-in-fact may be expected to attempt to deal with after the revocation.

DURABLE UNLIMITED POWER OF ATTORNEY

I, _____, residing at _____, City of _____, State of _____, grant an unlimited durable power of attorney to _____, residing at _____, City of _____, State of _____, to act as my attorney-in-fact.

I give my attorney-in-fact the maximum power under law to perform any acts on my behalf that I could do personally, including the power to make any health decisions on my behalf. My attorney-in-fact accepts this appointment and agrees to act in my best interest as he or she considers advisable. This power of attorney may be revoked by me at any time and is automatically revoked on my death. This power of attorney shall not be affected by my present or future disability or incapacity.

Dated: _____, 19 _____

_____
(Signature of person granting power of attorney)

State of _____
County of _____
On _____, 19 __, _____ came before me personally and, under oath, stated that he/she is the person described in the above document and he/she signed the above document in my presence.

_____
(Notary signature)

Notary Public, for the County of _____, State of _____
My commission expires: _____

I accept my appointment as attorney-in-fact.

_____
(Signature of person granted power of attorney)

DURABLE LIMITED POWER OF ATTORNEY

I, _____, residing at _____, City of _____, State of _____, grant a limited durable power of attorney to _____, residing at _____, City of _____, State of _____, to act as my attorney-in-fact.

I give my attorney-in-fact the maximum power under law to perform the following specific acts on my behalf:

My attorney-in-fact accepts this appointment and agrees to act in my best interest as he or she considers advisable. This power of attorney may be revoked by me at any time and is automatically revoked on my death. This power of attorney shall not be affected by my present or future disability or incapacity.

Dated: _____, 19 _____

_____
(Signature of person granting power of attorney)

State of _____
County of _____
On _____, 19 __, _____ came before me personally and, under oath, stated that he/she is the person described in the above document and he/she signed the above document in my presence.

_____
(Notary signature)

Notary Public, for the County of _____, State of _____
My commission expires: _____

I accept my appointment as attorney-in-fact.

_____
(Signature of person granted power of attorney)

REVOCATION OF POWER OF ATTORNEY

I, _____, residing at _____, City of _____, State of _____, revoke the Power of Attorney dated _____, 19 __, which was granted to _____, residing at _____, City of _____, State of _____, to act as my attorney-in-fact.

Dated: _____, 19 _____

_____
(Signature of person revoking power of attorney)

State of _____
County of _____

On _____, 19 __, _____ came before me personally and, under oath, stated that he/she is the person described in the above document and he/she signed the above document in my presence.

_____
(Notary signature)

Notary Public, for the County of _____, State of _____
My commission expires: _____

Appendix

State Laws Relating To Wills

The following listing contains a compilation of state laws relating to wills for all fifty states and the District of Columbia. It is recommended that you review the listing which pertains to your home state and any state in which you own real estate before you complete your will. The will clauses used in this book are generally designed to overcome and eliminate most potential legal problems raised by any of these individual state laws. There may, however, be some information which will directly affect the manner in which you decide to prepare your will.

As you review your state's particular laws, keep in mind that your will is going to be interpreted under the laws of the state in which you reside at the time of your death. Your personal property will be distributed according to the laws of the state in which you were a resident at the time of your death. Your real estate, however, will be distributed under the laws of the state in which it is located, regardless of where you are a resident.

Every effort has been made to insure that this list is as complete and up-to-date as possible. However, state laws are subject to change. While most laws relating to wills are relatively stable, it is advisable to check your particular state statutes to be certain there have been no major modifications since this book was prepared. To simplify this process as much as possible, the statute book description of each state's laws has been included in the following list. By using this description, you may easily locate the appropriate laws at your local library. If you have any difficulty, your local librarian will be glad to help. Be forewarned, however, that most legislators are lawyers and that, therefore, much of your state's statutes will be written in a difficult-to-understand legal jargon. Use the Glossary located at the end of this book to translate this language.

The state-by-state listings in this Appendix contain the following information for each state:

State law description: This listing contains a brief description of the state law book and chapter or section number listing where most of the relevant state laws on wills and probate are contained.

Court with probate jurisdiction: This listing provides the name of the particular court in each state which has exclusive jurisdiction over probate and will-related legal matters.

Minimum age for disposing of property by will: This listing details the minimum age for having a legally-valid will. For most states, this age is 18, but there are a few states that have differing laws.

Required number of witnesses: For most states, the minimum number of required witnesses is two. Be advised, however, that it is recommended to use at least three witnesses for your will.

May witnesses be beneficiaries?: Under this listing is information regarding whether witnesses to the signing of the will may be beneficiaries under the will. Again, be advised that, to be safe, your witnesses should *not* be beneficiaries.

Are there provisions for Self-Proving wills?: This listing details whether there are specific state law provisions for self-proving wills. To be prudent, for all wills (except in Louisiana), you are advised to use the Self-Proving Affidavit provided at the end of the will clauses in Chapter 6.

Are living wills recognized: Under this listing, the name of any relevant state laws regarding living wills is shown. However, for residents in those few states that have not yet enacted laws recognizing living wills, it is still recommended that you prepare one.

How does divorce affect the will?: The effect of divorce on the will under state law is shown in this listing. State law varies widely on this point and in some states a divorce may automatically revoke your entire will. It is highly recommended that you review and update your will if you are ever divorced.

How does marriage affect the will?: This listing provides the state law on the effect of marriage on the will. Again, state law provides various provisions and marriage may have the drastic effect of entirely revoking your will. It is, therefore, recommended that you review and update your will if you are ever married.

Who must be mentioned in the will?: Under this listing is shown which parties must be specifically mentioned in the will. Certain parties must be mentioned in your will or they may be entitled to an intestate share of your estate regardless of your will. Most states provide this protection for children born after a will is made and for new spouses from a marriage that takes place after a will is prepared. However, it is recommended that you review and change your will if you adopt or have any new children, are married, or if any of your named beneficiaries die.

Spouse's right to property regardless of will: This listing provides the results of a spouse's right of election against the will. In all states, the surviving spouse has a right to a certain share of the deceased spouse's estate regardless of any provisions in the will of the deceased spouse which may give him or her less that this "statutory" or "community" property share.

Laws of intestate distribution (distribution if decedent leaves no will): Under this listing the complex state provisions regarding intestate distribution of estates are outlined. This provides an overview of how your property would be distributed in the event that you die without a valid will. The laws in this area are extremely complex and differ widely from state to state. The outline of laws shown in this listing is intended to provide a simplified example of the particular state distribution scheme. If specific details of your state's distribution plan are needed, please consult the state statute directly.

A few definitions may be useful in deciphering the information listed in this section. The terms *per capita* and *per stirpes* are often used in these state plans. Per capita refers to a distribution to each member of a group equally. Per stirpes means distribution to a lower level group based on "representation" in the upper level. For example, a parent has 2 children, each of which have 2 grandchildren for a total of 6 descendents. However, one of the children died before the parent, leaving only 5 descendents. When the parent dies, a per capita distribution would divide the estate into 5 equal shares, with each descendent taking 1/5. In a per stirpes distribution, the estate is divided into 2 equal halves; one for each original child's share. The living child takes 1/2 and the grandchildren who are children of the deceased child each take 1/4. In effect, they share by "representation" their deceased parent's share of the estate. The grandchildren who are children of the living child would take nothing under a per stirpes distribution.

Another definition which may be useful is a *life estate*. A life estate in real estate is provided to the surviving spouse in some states upon a spouse's death. A life estate means that the surviving spouse has the full use and enjoyment of any real estate for her or his entire life. However, upon her or his death, the property will pass automatically to the person who has the remaining share of the estate. Most often this will be a child of the original deceased. The spouse who is given a life estate can not leave such a property interest to anyone else.

Community Property or Common Law state?: Whether the state follows the community property or common law system of ownership of marital property is shown in this listing.

State restrictions on gifts to charities?: This listing notes whether the state has restrictions on after-death gifts to charities. If your state has such restrictions, and you are contemplating a significant gift to a church or charity, please consult with an attorney.

State gift, inheritance, or estate taxes: This listing shows the tax situation in each state as it relates to estates and wills. There are three basic taxes that apply: gift taxes, inheritance taxes, and estate taxes. Each individual state may impose any of these taxes. Only one state, Nevada, does not impose any of these taxes.

Alabama

State law description: Code of Alabama; Title 43, Chapters 2-1 to 8-298.

Court with probate jurisdiction: Probate Court.

Minimum age for disposing of property by will: 18.

Required number of witnesses: Two. (Three are recommended).

May witnesses be beneficiaries?: Yes. (Not recommended).

Are there provisions for Self-Proving wills?: Yes. (Use the Self-Proving Affidavit in Chapter 6).

Are living wills recognized?: Yes, under the "Alabama Natural Death Act". (Use the living Will form in Chapter 12).

How does divorce affect the will?: Revokes the will as to the divorced spouse, unless expressly provided otherwise.

How does marriage affect the will?: Revokes the will as to the spouse if she or he is not otherwise provided for. Spouse may still be entitled to her or his statutory share under the state intestate laws.

Who must be mentioned in the will?: Children, born or adopted; surviving spouse.

Spouse's right to property regardless of will: The surviving spouse is entitled to 1/3 of the "augmented" estate of the deceased spouse. In general, the "augmented" estate includes both the property that passes under the will and any other property that passes by other "non-will" transfers, such as under the terms of a living trust or a joint tenancy arrangement.

Laws of intestate distribution (distribution if decedent leaves no will):

Spouse and children of spouse surviving: $50,000 and 1/2 of balance of estate to spouse and 1/2 of balance to children.

Spouse and children not of spouse surviving: 1/2 to spouse and 1/2 to children.

Spouse, but no children or parent(s) surviving: All to spouse.

Spouse and parent(s), but no children surviving: $100,000 and 1/2 of balance to spouse and 1/2 of balance to parent(s).

Children, but no spouse surviving: All to children equally or to their children per stirpes.

Parent(s), but no spouse or children surviving: All to parents equally or the surviving parent.

No spouse, children, or parent(s) surviving: All to brothers and sisters per stirpes; then to grandparents or their children per stirpes; then to deceased spouse's next of kin.

Community Property or Common Law state?: Common Law.

State restrictions on gifts to charities?: No.

State gift, inheritance, or estate taxes: No gift tax; no inheritance tax; imposes state estate tax equal to federal credit for state death taxes.

Alaska

State law description: Alaska Statutes; Sections 13.06 +.

Court with probate jurisdiction: Superior Court.

Minimum age for disposing of property by will: 18.

Required number of witnesses: Two. (Three recommended).

May witnesses be beneficiaries?: Yes. (Not recommended).

Are there provisions for Self-Proving wills?: Yes. (Use the Affidavit in Chapter 6).

Are living wills recognized?: Yes, under the "Alaska Rights of Terminally Ill Act". (Use the living will form in Chapter 12).

How does divorce affect the will?: Revokes the will as to the divorced spouse, unless expressly provided otherwise.

How does marriage affect the will?: Revokes the will as to the spouse if she or he is not otherwise provided for. Spouse may still be entitled to her or his statutory share under the state intestate laws.

Who must be mentioned in the will ? Children, born or adopted; surviving spouse.

Spouse's right to property regardless of will: The surviving spouse is entitled to 1/3 of the "augmented" estate of the deceased spouse. In general, the "augmented" estate includes both the property that passes under the will and any other property that passes by other "non-will" transfers, such as under the terms of a living trust or a joint tenancy arrangement.

Laws of intestate succession (distribution if decedent leaves no will):

Spouse and children of spouse surviving: $50,000 and 1/2 of balance to spouse and 1/2 of balance to children or grandchildren per stirpes.

Spouse and children not of spouse surviving: 1/2 to spouse and 1/2 to children or grandchildren per stirpes.

Spouse, but no children or parent(s) surviving: All to spouse.

Spouse and parent(s), but no children surviving: $50,000 and 1/2 of balance to spouse and 1/2 of balance to parents.

Children, but no spouse surviving: All to children equally or to their children per stirpes.

Parent(s), but no spouse or children surviving: All to parents equally, or to the surviving parent.

No spouse, children, or parent(s) surviving: All to brothers and sisters per stirpes; or if none, 1/2 to paternal grandparents and their children per stirpes and 1/2 to maternal grandparents and their children per stirpes.

Community Property or Common Law state?: Common Law.

State restrictions on gifts to charities?: No.

State gift, inheritance, or estate taxes: No gift tax; no inheritance tax; imposes state estate tax equal to federal credit for state death taxes.

Arizona

State law description: Arizona Revised Statutes Annotated; Title 14, Chapters 1102+, Title 33, Chapters 601+.

Court with probate jurisdiction: Superior Court.

Minimum age for disposing of property by will: 18.

Required number of witnesses: Two. (Three recommended).

May witnesses be beneficiaries?: Yes. (Not recommended).

Are there provisions for Self-Proving wills?: Yes. (Use the Affidavit in Chapter 6).

Are living wills recognized?: Yes, under the "Arizona Medical Treatment Decision Act". (Use the living will form in Chapter 12).

How does divorce affect the will?: Revokes the will as to the divorced spouse, unless expressly provided otherwise.

How does marriage affect the will?: Revokes the will as to the spouse if she or he is not otherwise provided for. Spouse may still be entitled to her or his statutory share under the state intestate laws.

Who must be mentioned in the will?: Children, born or adopted; surviving spouse.

Spouse's right to property regardless of will: Community property right to 1/2 of the deceased spouse's "community" property.

Laws of intestate succession (distribution if decedent leaves no will):

Spouse and children of spouse surviving: All of decedent's separate property and 1/2 of decedent's community property to spouse and 1/2 of decedent's community property to children.

Spouse and children not of spouse surviving: 1/2 of decedent's separate property to spouse and 1/2 of decedent's separate property and all of decedents community property to children.

Spouse, but no children or parent(s) surviving: All to spouse.

Spouse and parent(s), but no children surviving: All to spouse.

Children, but no spouse surviving: All to children equally or to their children per stirpes.

Parent(s), but no spouse or children surviving: All to parents equally, or to the surviving parent.

No spouse, children, or parent(s) surviving: All to brothers and sisters per stirpes; or if none, to the next of kin.

Community Property or Common Law state?: Community Property.

State restrictions on gifts to charities?: No.

State gift, inheritance, or estate taxes: No gift tax; no inheritance tax; imposes state estate tax equal to federal credit for state death taxes.

Arkansas

State law description: Arkansas Code of 1987 Annotated; Title 28, Chapters 24-101 to 48-305.

Court with probate jurisdiction: Probate Court.

Minimum age for disposing of property by will: 18.

Required number of witnesses: Two. (Three recommended).

May witnesses be beneficiaries?: Yes, but still must have 2 other disinterested witnesses.

Are there provisions for Self-Proving wills?: Yes. (Use the Affidavit in Chapter 6).

Are living wills recognized?: Yes, under the "Arkansas Rights of the Terminally Ill or Permanently Unconscious Act". (Use the living will form in Chapter 12).

How does divorce affect the will?: Revokes the will as to the divorced spouse.

How does marriage affect the will?: Does not revoke the will.

Who must be mentioned in the will ?: Children, born or adopted; surviving spouse.

Spouse's right to property regardless of will: Intestate share: 1/3 of personal property and 1/3 of real estate for life.

Laws of intestate succession (distribution if decedent leaves no will):

Spouse and children of spouse surviving: Real estate: 1/3 life estate to spouse and 2/3 to children equally or their children per stirpes; personal property: 1/3 to spouse and 2/3 to children equally or their children per stirpes.

Spouse and children not of spouse surviving: Real estate: 1/3 life estate to spouse and 2/3 to children equally or their children per stirpes; personal property: 1/3 to spouse and 2/3 to children equally or their children per stirpes.

Spouse, but no children or parent(s) surviving: All to spouse if married over 3 years. If married less than 3 years, 1/2 to spouse and 1/2 to brothers and sisters equally or their children per stripes; or if none, then to ancestors (up to great-grandparents; or if none, all to spouse.

Spouse and parent(s), but no children surviving: All to spouse if married over 3 years. If married less than 3 years, 1/2 to spouse and 1/2 to parent(s).

Children, but no spouse surviving: All to children equally or to their children per capita.

Parent(s), but no spouse or children surviving: All to parents equally, or to the surviving parent.

No spouse, children, or parent(s) surviving: All to brothers and sisters per stripes; or if none, to grandparents, and their children per stirpes.

Community Property or Common Law state?: Common Law.

State restrictions on gifts to charities?: No.

State gift, inheritance, or estate taxes: No gift tax; no inheritance tax; imposes state estate tax equal to federal credit for state death taxes.

California

State law description: Annotated California Code; Probate Code; Sections 6100+.

Court with probate jurisdiction: Superior Court.

Minimum age for disposing of property by will: 18.

Required number of witnesses: Two. (Three are recommended).

May witnesses be beneficiaries?: No.

Are there provisions for Self-Proving wills?: Yes. (Use the Affidavit in Chapter 6).

Are living wills recognized?: Yes, under the "California Natural Death Act". (Use the living will form in Chapter 12).

How does divorce affect the will?: Revoke the will as to divorced spouse , unless expressly provided otherwise.

How does marriage affect the will?: Revokes the will as to the surviving spouse.

Who must be mentioned in the will?: Children, born or adopted; grandchildren of deceased child; surviving spouse.

Spouse's right to property regardless of will: Community property right to 1/2 of the deceased spouse's "community" property.

Laws of intestate succession (distribution if decedent leaves no will):

Spouse and children of spouse surviving: All of decedent's community property to spouse. If one child: 1/2 of decedent's separate property to spouse and 1/2 to child per stirpes. If more than one child: 1/3 of decedent's separate property to spouse and 2/3 to children per stirpes.

Spouse and children not of spouse surviving: Same as above "Spouse and children of spouse surviving".

Spouse, but no children or parent(s) surviving: All of decedent's community property to spouse. 1/2 of decedent's separate property to spouse and 1/2 of decedent's separate property to brothers and sisters equally or to their children per stirpes; or if none, all to spouse.

Spouse and parent(s), but no children surviving: All of decedent's community property to spouse. 1/2 of decedent's separate property to spouse and 1/2 of decedent's separate property to parent(s) or surviving parent.

Children, but no spouse surviving: All to children equally or to their children per stirpes.

Parent(s), but no spouse or children surviving: All to parents equally, or to the surviving parent.

No spouse, children, or parent(s) surviving: All to brothers and sisters per stirpes; or if none, to the next of kin.

Community Property or Common Law state?: Community Property.

State restrictions on gifts to charities?: No.

State gift, inheritance, or estate taxes: No gift tax; no inheritance tax; imposes state estate tax equal to federal credit for state death taxes.

Colorado

State law description: Colorado Revised Statutes Annotated; Sections 15-10-101+, 15-11-101+, 15-12-101+.

Court with probate jurisdiction: District Court (Probate Court in Denver).

Minimum age for disposing of property by will: 18.

Required number of witnesses: Two. (Three are recommended).

May witnesses be beneficiaries?: Yes. (Not recommended).

Are there provisions for Self-Proving wills?: Yes. (Use the Affidavit in Chapter 6).

Are living wills recognized?: Yes, under the "Colorado Medical Treatment Decision Act" . (Use the living will form in Chapter 12).

How does divorce affect the will?: Revokes the will as to the divorced spouse.

How does marriage affect the will?: Revokes the will as to the spouse if she or he is not otherwise provided for. Spouse may still be entitled to her or his statutory share under the state intestate laws.

Who must be mentioned in the will ?: Children, born or adopted; surviving spouse.

Spouse's right to property regardless of will: The surviving spouse is entitled to 1/2 of the "augmented" estate of the deceased spouse. In general, the "augmented" estate includes both the property that passes under the will and any other property that passes by other "non-will" transfers, such as under the terms of a living trust or a joint tenancy arrangement.

Laws of intestate succession (distribution if decedent leaves no will):

Spouse and children of spouse surviving: $25,000 and 1/2 of balance to spouse and 1/2 of balance to children and grandchildren per stirpes.

Spouse and children not of spouse surviving: 1/2 to spouse and 1/2 to children and grandchildren per stirpes.

Spouse, but no children or parent(s) surviving: All to spouse.

Spouse and parent(s), but no children surviving: All to spouse.

Children, but no spouse surviving: All to children equally or to their children per stirpes.

Parent(s), but no spouse or children surviving: All to parents equally, or to the surviving parent.

No spouse, children, or parent(s) surviving: All to brothers and sisters per stirpes; or if none, to grandparents and their children per stirpes; or if none to nearest lineal ancestors and their children.

Community Property or Common Law state?: Common Law.

State restrictions on gifts to charities?: No.

State gift, inheritance, or estate taxes: No gift tax; no inheritance tax; imposes state estate tax equal to federal credit for state death taxes.

Connecticut

State law description: Connecticut General Statutes Annotated; Title 45a, Chapters 802+.

Court with probate jurisdiction: Probate Court.

Minimum age for disposing of property by will: 18.

Required number of witnesses: Two. (Three are recommended).

May witnesses be beneficiaries?: Yes, but must still have 2 other disinterested witnesses (or if witness/beneficiary is heir of testator).

Are there provisions for Self-Proving wills?: Yes. (Use the Affidavit in Chapter 6).

Are living wills recognized?: Yes, under the "Connecticut Removal of Life Support Systems Act". (Use the living will form in Chapter 12).

How does divorce affect the will?: Revokes the will completely, unless spouse was not a beneficiary under the will.

How does marriage affect the will?: Revokes the will completely, unless spouse was not a beneficiary under the will.

Who must be mentioned in the will?: Children, born or adopted; surviving spouse.

Spouse's right to property regardless of will: The surviving spouse is entitled to 1/3 of the deceased spouse's real estate and personal property for the rest of his or her life.

Laws of intestate succession (distribution if decedent leaves no will):

Spouse and children of spouse surviving: $100,000 and 1/2 of balance to spouse and 1/2 of balance to children or grandchildren per stirpes.

Spouse and children not of spouse surviving: 1/2 to spouse and 1/2 to children or grandchildren per stirpes.

Spouse, but no children or parent(s) surviving: All to spouse.

Spouse and parent(s), but no children surviving: $100,000 and 3/4 of balance to spouse, 1/4 of balance to parents or surviving parent.

Children, but no spouse surviving: All to children equally or to their children per stirpes.

Parent(s), but no spouse or children surviving: All to parents equally, or to the surviving parent.

No spouse, children, or parent(s) surviving: All to brothers and sisters per stirpes; or if none, to next of kin.

Community Property or Common Law state?: Common Law.

State restrictions on gifts to charities?: No.

State gift, inheritance, or estate taxes: No gift tax; no inheritance tax; imposes state estate tax equal to federal credit for state death taxes.

Delaware

State law description: Delaware Code Annotated; Title 12, Chapters 101+.

Court with probate jurisdiction: Chancery Court.

Minimum age for disposing of property by will: 18.

Required number of witnesses: Two. (Three are recommended).

May witnesses be beneficiaries?: Yes. (Not recommended).

Are there provisions for Self-Proving wills?: Yes. (Use the Affidavit in Chapter 6).

Are living wills recognized?: Yes, under the "Delaware Death With Dignity Act". (Use the living will form in Chapter 12).

How does divorce affect the will?: Revokes the will as to the divorced spouse, unless expressly provided otherwise.

How does marriage affect the will?: Does not revoke the will.

Who must be mentioned in the will?: Children, born or adopted; surviving spouse.

Spouse's right to property regardless of will: The surviving spouse is entitled to 1/3 of the deceased spouse's estate or $20,000.00, whichever is less.

Laws of intestate succession (distribution if decedent leaves no will):

Spouse and children of spouse surviving: Real estate: Life estate to spouse; all the rest to children or grandchildren per stirpes; Personal property: $50,000 and 1/2 of balance to spouse and 1/2 of balance to children or grandchildren per stirpes.

Spouse and children not of spouse surviving: Real estate: Life estate to spouse; all the rest to children or grandchildren per stirpes; Personal property: 1/2 to spouse and 1/2 to children or grandchildren per stirpes.

Spouse, but no children or parent(s) surviving: All to spouse.

Spouse and parent(s), but no children surviving: Real estate: Life estate to spouse; all the rest to parents or surviving parent; Personal property: $50,000 and 1/2 of balance to spouse and 1/2 of balance to parents or surviving parent.

Children, but no spouse surviving: All to children equally or to their children per stirpes.

Parent(s), but no spouse or children surviving: All to parents equally, or to the surviving parent.

No spouse, children, or parent(s) surviving: All to brothers or sisters or their children per stirpes; or if none, to the next of kin.

Community Property or Common Law state?: Common Law.

State restrictions on gifts to charities?: No.

State gift, inheritance, or estate taxes: Imposes a state gift tax; imposes an inheritance tax of up to 16%; imposes state estate tax equal to federal credit for state death taxes less any amounts paid on state inheritance tax. Maximum total state inheritance and state estate tax is equal to the maximum allowable federal estate tax credit for state death taxes.

District Of Columbia (Washington D.C.)

State law description: District of Columbia Code Annotated; Sections 16-101+, 18-101+, 20-101+, 45-101+.
Court with probate jurisdiction: Superior Court.
Minimum age for disposing of property by will: 18.
Required number of witnesses: Two. (Three are recommended).
May witnesses be beneficiaries?: No.
Are there provisions for Self-Proving wills?: Yes. (Use the Affidavit in Chapter 6).
Are living wills recognized?: Yes, under the "District of Columbia Natural Death Act". (Use the living will form in Chapter 12).
How does divorce affect the will?: Generally, revokes the will.
How does marriage affect the will?: Generally, revokes the will.
Who must be mentioned in the will?: Surviving spouse.
Spouse's right to property regardless of will: The surviving spouse is entitled to 1/3 of the deceased spouse's real estate for the rest of his or her life.
Laws of intestate succession (distribution if decedent leaves no will):
  Spouse and children of spouse surviving: Real estate: 1/3 life estate to spouse and balance to children equally or their children per stirpes; Personal property: 1/3 to spouse and 2/3 to children equally or their children per stirpes.
  Spouse and children not of spouse surviving: Real estate: 1/3 life estate to spouse and balance to children equally or their children per stirpes; Personal property: 1/3 to spouse and 2/3 to children equally or their children per stirpes.
  Spouse, but no children or parent(s) surviving: Real estate: 1/3 life estate to spouse and balance to parent's children per stirpes; or if none, to collaterals; or if none, to grandparents; or if none, all to spouse; Personal property: 1/2 to spouse and 1/2 to parent's children per stirpes; or if none, to collaterals; or if none, to grandparents; or if none, all to spouse.
  Spouse and parent(s), but no children surviving: Real estate: 1/3 life estate to spouse and balance to parents or surviving parent; Personal property: 1/2 to spouse and 1/2 to parents or surviving parent.
  Children, but no spouse surviving: All to children equally or to their children per stirpes.
  Parent(s), but no spouse or children surviving: All to parents equally, or to the surviving parent.
  No spouse, children, or parent(s) surviving: All to brothers and sisters or their children per stirpes; or if none, to collaterals; or if none, to grandparents.
Community Property or Common Law state?: Common Law.
State restrictions on gifts to charities?: No.
State gift, inheritance, or estate taxes: No gift tax; no inheritance tax; imposes state estate tax equal to federal credit for state death taxes.

Florida

State law description: Florida Statutes Annotated; Chapters 731.005+, 732.501+, 733.101+.

Court with probate jurisdiction: Circuit Court.

Minimum age for disposing of property by will: 18.

Required number of witnesses: Two. (Three are recommended).

May witnesses be beneficiaries?: Yes. (Not recommended).

Are there provisions for Self-Proving wills?: Yes. (Use the Affidavit in Chapter 6).

Are living wills recognized?: Yes, under the "Life Prolonging Procedure Act of Florida". (Use the living will form in Chapter 12).

How does divorce affect the will?: Revokes the will as to the divorced spouse.

How does marriage affect the will?: Revokes the will as to the spouse if she or he is not otherwise provided for. Spouse will still be entitled to her or his statutory share under the state intestate laws, regardless of prior will.

Who must be mentioned in the will?: Children, born or adopted; surviving spouse.

Spouse's right to property regardless of will: The surviving spouse is entitled to 30% of the deceased spouse's estate.

Laws of intestate succession (distribution if decedent leaves no will):

Spouse and children of spouse surviving: $20,000 and 1/2 of balance to spouse and 1/2 of balance to children and grandchildren per stirpes.

Spouse and children not of spouse surviving: 1/2 to spouse and 1/2 to children and grandchildren per stirpes.

Spouse, but no children or parent(s) surviving: All to spouse.

Spouse and parent(s), but no children surviving: All to spouse.

Children, but no spouse surviving: All to children equally or to their children per stirpes.

Parent(s), but no spouse or children surviving: All to parents equally, or to the surviving parent.

No spouse, children, or parent(s) surviving: All to brothers and sisters or their children per stirpes; or if none, 1/2 to maternal next of kin and 1/2 to paternal next of kin beginning with grandparents.

Community Property or Common Law state?: Common Law.

State restrictions on gifts to charities?: Yes. If extensive gifts to charities are contemplated, please refer directly to statute or consult an attorney.

State gift, inheritance, or estate taxes: No gift tax; no inheritance tax; imposes state estate tax equal to federal credit for state death taxes.

Georgia

State law description: Code of Georgia Annotated; Title 24, Sections 101+, Title 113, Sections 101+.

Court with probate jurisdiction: Probate Court.

Minimum age for disposing of property by will: 14.

Required number of witnesses: Two. (Three are recommended).

May witnesses be beneficiaries?: Yes, but any gift to witness who is a beneficiary is void unless there were also two other disinterested witnesses.

Are there provisions for Self-Proving wills?: Yes. (Use the Affidavit in Chapter 6).

Are living wills recognized?: Yes, under the "Georgia Living Wills Act". (Use the living will form in Chapter 12).

How does divorce affect the will?: Revokes the will completely, unless expressly provided otherwise.

How does marriage affect the will?: Revokes the will completely, unless expressly provided otherwise.

Who must be mentioned in the will?: Statute contains detailed provisions regarding this matter. Please refer directly to statute text or consult an attorney if this is a critical factor.

Spouse's right to property regardless of will: The surviving spouse is entitled to one year's support from the deceased spouse's estate.

Laws of intestate succession (distribution if decedent leaves no will):

Spouse and children of spouse surviving: Children or grandchildren and spouse all take equal shares, with at least 1/4 to spouse.

Spouse and children not of spouse surviving: Children or grandchildren and spouse all take equal shares, with at least 1/4 to spouse.

Spouse, but no children or parent(s) surviving: All to spouse.

Spouse and parent(s), but no children surviving: All to spouse.

Children, but no spouse surviving: All to children equally or to their children per stirpes.

Parent(s), but no spouse or children surviving: All to parents, brothers and sisters equally, or to their children per stirpes.

No spouse, children, or parent(s) surviving: All to brothers and sisters or their children per stirpes; or if none, to paternal and maternal next of kin.

Community Property or Common Law state?: Common Law.

State restrictions on gifts to charities?: Yes. If extensive gifts to charities are contemplated, please refer directly to statute or consult an attorney.

State gift, inheritance, or estate taxes: No gift tax; no inheritance tax; imposes state estate tax equal to federal credit for state death taxes.

Hawaii

State law description: Hawaii Revised Statutes; Title 560, Sections 2+.

Court with probate jurisdiction: Circuit Court.

Minimum age for disposing of property by will: 18.

Required number of witnesses: Two. (Three are recommended).

May witnesses be beneficiaries?: Yes. (Not recommended).

Are there provisions for Self-Proving wills?: Yes. (Use the Affidavit in Chapter 6).

Are living wills recognized?: Yes, under the "Hawaii Medical Treatment Decisions Act". (Use the living will form in Chapter 12).

How does divorce affect the will?: Revokes the will as to the divorced spouse, unless expressly provided otherwise.

How does marriage affect the will?: Revokes the will as to the spouse if she or he is not otherwise provided for. Spouse may still be entitled to her or his statutory share under the state intestate laws.

Who must be mentioned in the will?: Children, born or adopted; surviving spouse.

Spouse's right to property regardless of will: The surviving spouse is entitled to 1/3 of the deceased spouse's estate.

Laws of intestate succession (distribution if decedent leaves no will):

Spouse and children of spouse surviving: 1/2 to spouse and 1/2 to children equally or to the grandchildren.

Spouse and children not of spouse surviving: 1/2 to spouse and 1/2 to children equally or to the grandchildren.

Spouse, but no children or parent(s) surviving: All to spouse.

Spouse and parent(s), but no children surviving: 1/2 to spouse and 1/2 to parents or surviving parent.

Children, but no spouse surviving: All to children equally or to their children per stirpes.

Parent(s), but no spouse or children surviving: All to parents equally, or to the surviving parent.

No spouse, children, or parent(s) surviving: All to brothers and sisters or their children per stirpes; or if none, to grandparents; or if none, to uncles and aunts equally.

Community Property or Common Law state?: Common Law.

State restrictions on gifts to charities?: No.

State gift, inheritance, or estate taxes: No gift tax; no inheritance tax; imposes state estate tax equal to federal credit for state death taxes.

Idaho

State law description: Idaho Code; Title 15, Chapter 1+.

Court with probate jurisdiction: District Court.

Minimum age for disposing of property by will: 18, or emancipated from parents.

Required number of witnesses: Two. (Three are recommended).

May witnesses be beneficiaries?: Yes. (Not recommended).

Are there provisions for Self-Proving wills?: Yes. (Use the Affidavit in Chapter 6).

Are living wills recognized?: Yes, under the "Idaho Natural Death Act". (Use the living will form in Chapter 12).

How does divorce affect the will?: Revokes the will as to the divorced spouse, unless expressly provided otherwise.

How does marriage affect the will?: Revokes the will as to the spouse if she or he is not otherwise provided for. Spouse may still be entitled to her or his statutory share under the state intestate laws.

Who must be mentioned in the will?: Children, born or adopted; surviving spouse.

Spouse's right to property regardless of will: Community property right to 1/2 of the deceased spouse's "community" property.

Laws of intestate succession (distribution if decedent leaves no will):

Spouse and children of spouse surviving: All of decedent's community property to spouse; $50,000 and 1/2 of balance of decedent's separate property to spouse and 1/2 of balance to children or grandchildren per stirpes.

Spouse and children not of spouse surviving: All of decedent's community property to spouse; 1/2 of decedent's separate property to spouse and 1/2 to children or grandchildren per stirpes.

Spouse, but no children or parent(s) surviving: All to spouse.

Spouse and parent(s), but no children surviving: All of decedent's community property to spouse; $50,000 and 1/2 of balance of decedent's separate property to spouse and 1/2 of balance to parents or surviving parent.

Children, but no spouse surviving: All to children or to their children per stirpes.

Parent(s), but no spouse or children surviving: All to parents equally, or to the surviving parent.

No spouse, children, or parent(s) surviving: All to brothers and sisters or their children, if surviving. If not, then 1/2 to living maternal grandparents or their children and 1/2 to paternal grandparents or their children.

Community Property or Common Law state?: Community Property.

State restrictions on gifts to charities?: Yes. If extensive gifts to charities are contemplated, please refer directly to statute or consult an attorney.

State gift, inheritance, or estate taxes: No gift tax; imposes an inheritance tax of up to 30%; imposes state estate tax equal to federal credit for state death taxes less any amounts paid on state inheritance tax. Maximum total state inheritance and state estate tax is equal to the maximum allowable federal estate tax credit for state death taxes.

Illinois

State law description: Illinois Compiled Statutes; 755 ILCS 5/1+.

Court with probate jurisdiction: Circuit Court.

Minimum age for disposing of property by will: 18.

Required number of witnesses: Two. (Three are recommended).

May witnesses be beneficiaries?: Yes, but any gift to a beneficiary who was a witness will be void unless there were also two other disinterested witnesses.

Are there provisions for Self-Proving wills?: Not in statutes. However self-proving affidavits have been accepted in the courts. (Use the Affidavit in Chapter 6).

Are living wills recognized?: Yes, under the "Illinois Living Wills and Life-Prolonging Procedures Act". (Use the living will form in Chapter 12).

How does divorce affect the will?: Revokes the will as to the divorced spouse.

How does marriage affect the will?: Does not revoke the will.

Who must be mentioned in the will?: Children, born or adopted; surviving spouse.

Spouse's right to property regardless of will: Generally, the surviving spouse is entitled to 1/2 of the deceased spouse's estate if there are no children, and only 1/3 if there are children. However, please refer directly to the statute as the provisions are detailed.

Laws of intestate succession (distribution if decedent leaves no will):

Spouse and children of spouse surviving: 1/2 to spouse and 1/2 to children equally or to the grandchildren per stirpes.

Spouse and children not of spouse surviving: 1/2 to spouse and 1/2 to children equally or to the grandchildren per stirpes.

Spouse, but no children or parent(s) surviving: All to spouse.

Spouse and parent(s), but no children surviving: All to spouse.

Children, but no spouse surviving: All to children equally or to their children per stirpes.

Parent(s), but no spouse or children surviving: All to parents, brothers, sisters, or children of brother and sisters per stirpes. If only one surviving parent, they take a double share.

No spouse, children, or parent(s) surviving: 1/2 to maternal and 1/2 to paternal grandparents equally or to surviving grandparent; or if none, to their children per stirpes; or if none, 1/2 to maternal and 1/2 to paternal great-grandparents equally or to surviving great-grandparent; or if none, to their children per stirpes; or if none of the above, all to the next of kin.

Community Property or Common law state?: Common Law.

State restrictions on gifts to charities?: No.

State gift, inheritance, or estate taxes: No gift tax; no inheritance tax; imposes state estate tax equal to federal credit for state death taxes.

Indiana

State law description: Indiana Code Annotated; Title 29, Chapters 1-1+.

Court with probate jurisdiction: Circuit or Superior Court (Probate Court in St. Joseph and Vigo Counties).

Minimum age for disposing of property by will: 18, or member of Armed Forces or Merchant Marine.

Required number of witnesses: Two. (Three are recommended).

May witnesses be beneficiaries?: Yes, but any gift to a beneficiary who was a witness will be void unless there were also two other disinterested witnesses.

Are there provisions for Self-Proving wills?: Yes. (Use the Affidavit in Chapter 6).

Are living wills recognized?: Yes, under the "Indiana Living Wills and Life-Prolonging Procedures Act". (Use the living will form in Chapter 12).

How does divorce affect the will?: Revokes the will as to the divorced spouse.

How does marriage affect the will?: Does not revoke the will.

Who must be mentioned in the will?: Children, born or adopted; surviving spouse.

Spouse's right to property regardless of will: The surviving spouse is entitled to 1/2 of the deceased spouse's estate. If there are surviving children of a prior spouse, a second or subsequent spouse is entitled to 1/3 of the deceased's personal property and 1/3 of the deceased's real estate for the rest of her life.

Laws of intestate succession (distribution if decedent leaves no will):

Spouse and children of spouse surviving: 1/2 to spouse and 1/2 to children.

Spouse and children not of spouse surviving: Real estate: life estate of 1/3 of real estate to spouse, balance to children; Personal property: 1/3 to spouse and 2/3 to children.

Spouse, but no children or parent(s) surviving: All to spouse.

Spouse and parent(s), but no children surviving: 3/4 to spouse and 1/4 to parents or surviving parent.

Children, but no spouse surviving: All to children equally or to their children per stirpes.

Parent(s), brothers, sisters, and children of brothers and sisters, but no spouse or children surviving: Surviving parents, brothers, sisters all share equally, but parents entitled to at least 1/4 of estate.

No spouse, children, parent(s), or brothers or sisters surviving: All to brothers and sisters children per stirpes; or if none, to grandparents; or if none, to aunts and uncles per stirpes.

Community Property or Common Law state?: Common Law.

State restrictions on gifts to charities?: No.

State gift, inheritance, or estate taxes: No gift tax; imposes an inheritance tax of up to 20%; imposes state estate tax equal to federal credit for state death taxes less any amounts paid on state inheritance tax. Maximum total state inheritance and state estate tax is equal to the maximum allowable federal estate tax credit for state death taxes.

Iowa

State law description: Iowa Code Annotated; Sections 633.1+.

Court with probate jurisdiction: District Court.

Minimum age for disposing of property by will: 18.

Required number of witnesses: Two. (Three are recommended).

May witnesses be beneficiaries?: Yes, but any gift to a beneficiary who was a witness will be void unless there were also two other disinterested witnesses.

Are there provisions for Self-Proving wills?: Yes. (Use the Affidavit in Chapter 6).

Are living wills recognized?: Yes, under the "Iowa Life Sustaining Procedures Act". (Use the living will form in Chapter 12).

How does divorce affect the will?: Revokes the will as to divorced spouse, unless they remarry.

How does marriage affect the will?: Revokes the will as to the spouse if she or he is not otherwise provided for. Spouse may still be entitled to her or his statutory share under the state intestate laws.

Who must be mentioned in the will?: Children, born or adopted; surviving spouse.

Spouse's right to property regardless of will: The surviving spouse is entitled to 1/3 of the deceased spouse's estate.

Laws of intestate succession (distribution if decedent leaves no will):

Spouse and children of spouse surviving: All to spouse.

Spouse and children not of spouse surviving: $50,000 and 1/2 of balance to spouse and 1/2 of balance to children.

Spouse, but no children or parent(s) surviving: All to spouse.

Spouse and parent(s), but no children surviving: All to spouse.

Children, but no spouse surviving: All to children equally or to their children per stirpes.

Parent(s), but no spouse or children surviving: All to parents equally, or to the surviving parent.

No spouse, children, or parent(s) surviving: All to brothers and sisters or their children per stirpes; or if none, to ancestors and their children per stirpes; or if none, to spouse or heirs of spouse.

Community Property or Common Law state?: Common Law.

State restrictions on gifts to charities?: No.

State gift, inheritance, or estate taxes: No gift tax; imposes an inheritance tax of up to 15%; imposes state estate tax equal to federal credit for state death taxes less any amounts paid on state inheritance tax. Maximum total state inheritance and state estate tax is equal to the maximum allowable federal estate tax credit for state death taxes.

Kansas

State law description: Kansas Statutes Annotated; Chapter 59, Subjects Sections -101, 501+, 601+

Court with probate jurisdiction: District Court.

Minimum age for disposing of property by will: 18.

Required number of witnesses: Two. (Three are recommended).

May witnesses be beneficiaries?: No, unless witness would be entitled to an intestate share in the absence of a will.

Are there provisions for Self-Proving wills?: Yes. (Use the Affidavit in Chapter 6).

Are living wills recognized?: Yes, under the "Kansas Natural Death Act". (Use the living will form in Chapter 12).

How does divorce affect the will?: Revokes the will as to the divorced spouse.

How does marriage affect the will?: Revokes the will if a child is later born to or adopted into the marriage.

Who must be mentioned in the will?: Surviving spouse.

Spouse's right to property regardless of will: Generally, the surviving spouse is entitled to 1/2 of the deceased spouse's estate if there are no children, and only 1/3 if there are children. However, please refer directly to the statute as the provisions are detailed.

Laws of intestate succession (distribution if decedent leaves no will):

Spouse and children of spouse surviving: 1/2 to spouse and 1/2 to children or grandchildren per stirpes.

Spouse and children not of spouse surviving: 1/2 to spouse and 1/2 to children or grandchildren per stirpes.

Spouse, but no children or parent(s) surviving: All to spouse.

Spouse and parent(s), but no children surviving: All to spouse.

Children, but no spouse surviving: All to children equally or to their children per stirpes.

Parent(s), but no spouse or children surviving: All to parents equally, or to the surviving parent.

No spouse, children, or parent(s) surviving: All to brothers and sisters per stirpes.

Community Property or Common law state?: Common Law.

State restrictions on gifts to charities?: No.

State gift, inheritance, or estate taxes: No gift tax; imposes an inheritance tax of up to 15%; imposes state estate tax equal to federal credit for state death taxes less any amounts paid on state inheritance tax. Maximum total state inheritance and state estate tax is equal to the maximum allowable federal estate tax credit for state death taxes.

Kentucky

State law description: Kentucky Revised Statutes; Chapters 394.000+, 395.000+.

Court with probate jurisdiction: District Court.

Minimum age for disposing of property by will: 18.

Required number of witnesses: Two. (Three are recommended).

May witnesses be beneficiaries?: No.

Are there provisions for Self-Proving wills?: Yes. (Use the Affidavit in Chapter 6).

Are living wills recognized?: Yes, under the "Kentucky Living Will Act. (Use the living will form in Chapter 12).

How does divorce affect the will?: Revokes the will as to the divorced spouse.

How does marriage affect the will?: Revokes the will completely, unless expressly provided otherwise.

Who must be mentioned in the will?: Children, born or adopted; surviving spouse.

Spouse's right to property regardless of will: The surviving spouse is entitled to 1/3 of the deceased spouse's real estate for the rest of his or her life.

Laws of intestate succession (distribution if decedent leaves no will):

Spouse and children of spouse surviving: Real estate: life estate of 1/3 of fee simple property acquired during marriage and 1/2 of other real estate to spouse; balance to children or grandchildren per stirpes; Personal property: 1/2 to spouse and 1/2 to children equally or grandchildren per stirpes.

Spouse and children not of spouse surviving: Same as above for "Spouse and children of spouse surviving".

Spouse, but no children or parent(s) surviving: 1/2 to parents children; or if none, all to spouse.

Spouse and parent(s), but no children surviving: 1/2 to spouse and 1/2 to parents or surviving parent.

Children, but no spouse surviving: All to children equally or to their children per stirpes.

Parent(s), but no spouse or children surviving: All to parents equally, or to the surviving parent.

No spouse, children, or parent(s) surviving: All to brothers and sisters or their children per stirpes; or if none, 1/2 to maternal next of kin and 1/2 to paternal next of kin and their children per stirpes.

Community Property or Common Law state?: Common Law.

State restrictions on gifts to charities?: No.

State gift, inheritance, or estate taxes: No gift tax; imposes an inheritance tax of up to 16%; imposes state estate tax equal to federal credit for state death taxes less any amounts paid on state inheritance tax. Maximum total state inheritance and state estate tax is equal to the maximum allowable federal estate tax credit for state death taxes.

Louisiana

State law description: Louisiana Revised Statutes; Louisiana Civil Code Annotated.

Court with probate jurisdiction: District Court.

Minimum age for disposing of property by will: 16.

Required number of witnesses: Three.

May witnesses be beneficiaries?: No.

Are there provisions for Self-Proving wills?: Yes, but follow procedures in Chapter 9.

Are living wills recognized?: Yes, under the "Louisiana Natural Death Act". (Use the living will form in Chapter 12).

How does divorce affect the will?: Does not revoke the will.

How does marriage affect the will?: Does not revoke the will.

Who must be mentioned in the will?: Children, born or adopted; surviving spouse.

Spouse's right to property regardless of will: The Louisiana Civil Code provisions regarding this matter are detailed and should be consulted directly.

Laws of intestate succession (distribution if decedent leaves no will):

Spouse and children of spouse surviving: All community property to descendents per stirpes. However, the spouse has the right to use the property until remarried. All separate property to children equally or grandchildren per stirpes.

Spouse and children not of spouse surviving: Same as above for "Spouse and children of spouse surviving".

Spouse, but no children or parent(s) surviving: All community property to spouse; all separate property to brothers and sisters or their children per stirpes; or if none, to parents; or if none, all to spouse.

Spouse and parent(s), but no children surviving: All community property to spouse; all separate property to brothers and sisters or their children per stirpes; or if none, to parents; or if none, all to spouse.

Children, but no spouse surviving: All to children equally or to their children per stirpes.

Parent(s), but no spouse or children surviving: All to parents equally, or to the surviving parent.

No spouse, children, or parent(s) surviving: To brothers and sisters equally or their children per stirpes; or if none, to next of kin.

Community Property or Common Law state?: Community property based on the Louisiana Civil Code.

State restrictions on gifts to charities?: No.

State gift, inheritance, or estate taxes: Imposes a state gift tax; imposes an inheritance tax of up to 10%; imposes a state estate tax equal to federal credit for state death taxes less any amounts paid on state inheritance tax. Maximum total state inheritance and state estate tax is equal to the maximum allowable federal estate tax credit for state death taxes.

Maine

State law description: Maine Revised Statutes Annotated; Title 18-A, Sections 1-101+, 2-501+, 3-101+.

Court with probate jurisdiction: Probate Court.

Minimum age for disposing of property by will: 18, married, or a surviving spouse.

Required number of witnesses: Three.

May witnesses be beneficiaries?: Yes. (Not recommended).

Are there provisions for Self-Proving wills?: Yes. (Use the Affidavit in Chapter 6).

Are living wills recognized?: Yes, under the "Maine Living Will Act". (Use the living will form in Chapter 12).

How does divorce affect the will?: Revokes the will as to the divorced spouse.

How does marriage affect the will?: Revokes the will as to the spouse if she or he is not otherwise provided for. Spouse may still be entitled to her or his statutory share under the state intestate laws.

Who must be mentioned in the will?: Children, born or adopted; grandchildren of deceased child; surviving spouse.

Spouse's right to property regardless of will: The surviving spouse is entitled to 1/3 of the entire estate of the deceased spouse.

Laws of intestate succession (distribution if decedent leaves no will):

Spouse and children of spouse surviving: $50,000 and 1/2 of balance to spouse and 1/2 of balance to children or grandchildren per stirpes.

Spouse and children not of spouse surviving: 1/2 to spouse and 1/2 to children or grandchildren per stirpes.

Spouse, but no children or parent(s) surviving: All to spouse.

Spouse and parent(s), but no children surviving: $50,000 and 1/2 of balance to spouse and 1/2 of balance to parents or surviving parent.

Children, but no spouse surviving: All to children equally or to their children per stirpes.

Parent(s), but no spouse or children surviving: All to parents equally, or to the surviving parent.

No spouse, children, or parent(s) surviving: All to children of parents per capita, or if none then 1/2 to paternal grandparents or their children per capita and 1/2 to maternal grandparents or their children per capita.

Community Property or Common Law state?: Common Law.

State restrictions on gifts to charities?: No.

State gift, inheritance, or estate taxes: No gift tax; no inheritance tax; imposes state estate tax equal to federal credit for state death taxes.

Maryland

State law description: Maryland Code; Estates and Trusts, Title 3, Sections 3-101+.

Court with probate jurisdiction: Orphan's Court (Circuit Court in Hartford and Montgomery Counties).

Minimum age for disposing of property by will: 18.

Required number of witnesses: Two. (Three are recommended).

May witnesses be beneficiaries?: Yes. (Not recommended).

Are there provisions for Self-Proving wills?: Yes. (Use the Affidavit in Chapter 6).

Are living wills recognized?: Yes, under the "Maryland Life Sustaining Procedures Act". (Use the living will form in Chapter 12).

How does divorce affect the will?: Revokes the will as to the divorced spouse.

How does marriage affect the will?: Revokes the will if a child is later born to or adopted into the marriage and survives the maker of the will

Who must be mentioned in the will?: Children, born or adopted; grandchildren (of deceased child); surviving spouse.

Spouse's right to property regardless of will: Generally, the surviving spouse is entitled to 1/2 of the deceased spouse's estate if there are no children, and only 1/3 if there are children. However, please refer directly to the statute for details.

Laws of intestate succession (distribution if decedent leaves no will):

Spouse and children of spouse surviving: If any surviving children are minors, 1/2 to spouse and 1/2 to children equally or grandchildren per stirpes; if no surviving children are minors, $15,000 and 1/2 of balance to spouse and 1/2 of balance to children equally or grandchildren per stirpes.

Spouse and children not of spouse surviving: Same as above for "Spouse and children of spouse surviving".

Spouse, but no children or parent(s) surviving: All to spouse.

Spouse and parent(s), but no children surviving: 1st $15,000 to spouses and then 1/2 to spouse and 1/2 to parents or surviving parent.

Children, but no spouse surviving: All to children or to their children per stirpes.

Parent(s), but no spouse or children surviving: All to parents equally, or to the surviving parent.

No spouse, children, or parent(s) surviving: All to brothers and sisters equally or to their children per stirpes; or if none, 1/2 to paternal grandparents and 1/2 to maternal grandparents and their next of kin.

Community Property or Common law state?: Common Law.

State restrictions on gifts to charities?: No.

State gift, inheritance, or estate taxes: No gift tax; imposes an inheritance tax of up to 10%; imposes state estate tax equal to federal credit for state death taxes less any amounts paid on state inheritance tax. Maximum total state inheritance and state estate tax is equal to the maximum allowable federal estate tax credit for state death taxes.

Massachusetts

State law description: Massachusetts General Laws; Chapter 191, Sections 1+.

Court with probate jurisdiction: Probate and Family Court.

Minimum age for disposing of property by will: 18.

Required number of witnesses: Two. (Three are recommended).

May witnesses be beneficiaries?: Yes, but any gift to a beneficiary who was a witness will be void unless there were also two other disinterested witnesses.

Are there provisions for Self-Proving wills?: Yes. (Use the Affidavit in Chapter 6).

Are living wills recognized?: Not by statute. However, you may still use the living will form in Chapter 12.

How does divorce affect the will?: Revokes the will as to the divorced spouse.

How does marriage affect the will?: Revokes the will.

Who must be mentioned in the will?: Children, born or adopted; grandchildren (if of deceased child); surviving spouse.

Spouse's right to property regardless of will: Generally, the surviving spouse is entitled to $25,000.00 and 1/2 of the deceased spouse's remaining estate if there are no children, and only 1/3 if there are children. However, please refer directly to the statute as the provisions are detailed.

Laws of intestate succession (distribution if decedent leaves no will):

Spouse and children of spouse surviving: 1/2 to spouse and 1/2 to children equally or grandchildren per stirpes.

Spouse and children not of spouse surviving: 1/2 to spouse and 1/2 to children equally or grandchildren per stirpes.

Spouse, but no children or parent(s) surviving: $200,000 and 1/2 of balance to spouse and 1/2 of balance to brothers and sisters equally or their children per stirpes; or if none, to next of kin; or if none, all to spouse.

Spouse and parent(s), but no children surviving: $200,000 and 1/2 of balance to spouse and 1/2 of balance to parents equally or the surviving parent.

Children, but no spouse surviving: All to children equally or to their children per stirpes.

Parent(s), but no spouse or children surviving: All to parents equally, or to the surviving parent.

No spouse, children, or parent(s) surviving: All to brothers and sisters equally or their children per stirpes; or if none, to the next of kin.

Community Property or Common law state?: Common Law.

State restrictions on gifts to charities?: No.

State gift, inheritance, or estate taxes: No gift tax; no inheritance tax; imposes state estate tax of up to 16% (not tied to federal estate tax credit).

Michigan

State law description: Michigan Compiled Laws Annotated; Sections 600.801+, 700.121+.

Court with probate jurisdiction: Probate Court.

Minimum age for disposing of property by will: 18.

Required number of witnesses: Two. (Three are recommended).

May witnesses be beneficiaries?: Yes, but any gift to a beneficiary who was a witness will be void unless there were also two other disinterested witnesses.

Are there provisions for Self-Proving wills?: Yes. (Use the Affidavit in Chapter 6).

Are living wills recognized?: Not by statute. However, you may still use the living will form in Chapter 12.

How does divorce affect the will?: Revokes the will as to the divorced spouse.

How does marriage affect the will?: Revokes the will as to the spouse if she or he is not otherwise provided for. Spouse may still be entitled to her or his statutory share under the state intestate laws.

Who must be mentioned in the will?: Children, born or adopted; surviving spouse.

Spouse's right to property regardless of will: Generally, the surviving spouse is entitled to 1/2 of the deceased spouse's estate if there are no children, and only 1/3 if there are children. However, please refer directly to the statute as the provisions are detailed.

Laws of intestate succession (distribution if decedent leaves no will):

Spouse and children of spouse surviving: $60,000 and 1/2 of balance to spouse and 1/2 of balance to children per stirpes.

Spouse and children not of spouse surviving: 1/2 to spouse and 1/2 to children per stirpes.

Spouse, but no children or parent(s) surviving: All to spouse.

Spouse and parent(s), but no children surviving: $60,000 and 1/2 of balance to spouse and 1/2 of balance to parents or surviving parent.

Children, but no spouse surviving: All to children or to their children per stirpes.

Parent(s), but no spouse or children surviving: All to parents equally, or to the surviving parent.

No spouse, children, or parent(s) surviving: All to brothers and sisters equally or to their children per stirpes; or if none, 1/2 to maternal grandparents or their children per stirpes and 1/2 to paternal grandparents or their children per stirpes.

Community Property or Common Law state?: Common Law.

State restrictions on gifts to charities?: No.

State gift, inheritance, or estate taxes: No gift tax; imposes an inheritance tax of up to 17%; imposes state estate tax equal to federal credit for state death taxes less any amounts paid on state inheritance tax. Maximum total state inheritance and state estate tax is equal to the maximum allowable federal estate tax credit for state death taxes.

Minnesota

State law description: Minnesota Statutes Annotated; Chapters 524.1-101+.

Court with probate jurisdiction: Probate Court.

Minimum age for disposing of property by will: 18.

Required number of witnesses: Two. (Three are recommended).

May witnesses be beneficiaries?: Yes. (Not recommended).

Are there provisions for Self-Proving wills?: Yes. (Use the Affidavit in Chapter 6).

Are living wills recognized?: Yes, under the "Minnesota Adult Health Care Decisions Act". (Use the living will form in Chapter 12).

How does divorce affect the will?: Revokes the will as to the divorced spouse.

How does marriage affect the will?: Revokes the will as to the spouse if she or he is not otherwise provided for. Spouse may still be entitled to her or his statutory share under the state intestate laws.

Who must be mentioned in the will?: Children, born or adopted; grandchildren (if of deceased child); surviving spouse.

Spouse's right to property regardless of will: Generally, the surviving spouse is entitled to 1/2 of the deceased spouse's estate if there are no children, and only 1/3 if there are children. However, please refer directly to the statute as the provisions are detailed.

Laws of intestate succession (distribution if decedent leaves no will):

Spouse and children of spouse surviving: $70,000 and 1/2 of balance to spouse and 1/2 of balance to children or grandchildren per stirpes.

Spouse and children not of spouse surviving: 1/2 to spouse and 1/2 to children or grandchildren per stirpes.

Spouse, but no children surviving: All to spouse.

Spouse and parent(s), but no children surviving: 1/2 to spouse and 1/2 to parents.

Children, but no spouse surviving: All to children equally or to their children per stirpes.

Parent(s), but no spouse or children surviving: All to parents equally, or to the surviving parent.

No spouse, children, or parent(s) surviving: All to brothers and sisters equally or their children per stirpes; or if none, to the next of kin.

Community Property or Common Law state?: Common Law.

State restrictions on gifts to charities?: No.

State gift, inheritance, or estate taxes: No gift tax; no inheritance tax; imposes state estate tax equal to federal credit for state death taxes.

Mississippi

State law description: Mississippi Code Annotated; Title 91, Chapters 1-1+.

Court with probate jurisdiction: Chancery Court.

Minimum age for disposing of property by will: 18.

Required number of witnesses: Two. (Three are recommended).

May witnesses be beneficiaries?: No.

Are there provisions for Self-Proving wills?: Yes. (Use the Affidavit in Chapter 6).

Are living wills recognized?: Yes, under the "Mississippi Natural Death Act". (Use the living will form in Chapter 12).

How does divorce affect the will?: Does not revoke the will.

How does marriage affect the will?: Does not revoke the will.

Who must be mentioned in the will?: Children, born or adopted; surviving spouse.

Spouse's right to property regardless of will: Generally, the surviving spouse is entitled to 1/2 of the deceased spouse's estate if there are no children, and only 1/3 if there are children. However, please refer directly to the statute as the provisions are detailed.

Laws of intestate succession (distribution if decedent leaves no will):

Spouse and children of spouse surviving: Spouse and any surviving children or grandchildren each take equal shares.

Spouse and children not of spouse surviving: Spouse and any surviving children or grandchildren each take equal shares.

Spouse, but no children or parent(s) surviving: All to spouse.

Spouse and parent(s), but no children surviving: All to spouse.

Children, but no spouse surviving: All to children equally or to their children per stirpes.

Parent(s), but no spouse or children surviving: All to parents, brothers, and sisters equally, or to children of brothers and sisters per stirpes. If no brothers or sisters or children of brothers or sisters, all to parents equally or the surviving parent.

No spouse, children, or parent(s) surviving: All to brothers and sisters equally, or to their children per stirpes; or if none, to grandparents, uncles, and aunts equally, or to their children per stirpes; or if none, to the next of kin.

Community Property or Common Law state?: Common Law.

State restrictions on gifts to charities?: Yes. If extensive gifts to charities are contemplated, please refer directly to statute or consult an attorney.

State gift, inheritance, or estate taxes: No gift tax; no inheritance tax; imposes state estate tax of up to 16%. (state estate tax not tied to federal credit for state death taxes).

Missouri

State law description: Missouri Annotated Statutes; Sections 472.005+, 474.010+.

Court with probate jurisdiction: Circuit Court.

Minimum age for disposing of property by will: 18.

Required number of witnesses: Two. (Three are recommended).

May witnesses be beneficiaries?: No.

Are there provisions for Self-Proving wills?: Yes. (Use the Affidavit in Chapter 6).

Are living wills recognized?: Yes, under the "Missouri Life Support Declaration Act". (Use the living will form in Chapter 12).

How does divorce affect the will?: Revokes the will as to the divorced spouse.

How does marriage affect the will?: Spouse may still be entitled to her or his statutory share under the state intestate laws.

Who must be mentioned in the will?: Children, born or adopted; surviving spouse.

Spouse's right to property regardless of will: Generally, the surviving spouse is entitled to 1/2 of the deceased spouse's estate if there are no children, and only 1/3 if there are children. However, please refer directly to the statute as the provisions are detailed.

Laws of intestate succession (distribution if decedent leaves no will):

Spouse and children of spouse surviving: $20,000 and 1/2 of balance to spouse and 1/2 of balance to children or grandchildren per stirpes.

Spouse and children not of spouse surviving: 1/2 to spouse and 1/2 to children or grandchildren per stirpes.

Spouse, but no children or parent(s) surviving: All to spouse.

Spouse and parent(s), but no children surviving: $20,000 and 1/2 of balance to spouse and 1/2 of balance to parents or surviving parent and brothers and sisters, per stirpes.

Children, but no spouse surviving: All to children equally or to their children per stirpes.

Parent(s), but no spouse or children surviving: All to parents, brothers, and sisters equally, or to their children per stirpes; or if none, all to parents or to the surviving parent.

No spouse, children, or parent(s) surviving: All to brothers and sisters equally or to their children per stirpes; or if none, to grandparents, uncles, and aunts and their children per stirpes; or if none, to the nearest lineal ancestor and their children.

Community Property or Common Law state?: Common Law.

State restrictions on gifts to charities?: No.

State gift, inheritance, or estate taxes: No gift tax; no inheritance tax; imposes state estate tax equal to federal credit for state death taxes.

Montana

State law description: Montana Code Annotated; Sections 72, Titles 1-101+.

Court with probate jurisdiction: District Court.

Minimum age for disposing of property by will: 18.

Required number of witnesses: Two. (Three are recommended).

May witnesses be beneficiaries?: Yes.

Are there provisions for Self-Proving wills?: Yes. (Use the Affidavit in Chapter 6).

Are living wills recognized?: Yes, under the "Montana Living Will Act". (Use the living will form in Chapter 12).

How does divorce affect the will?: Revokes the will as to the divorced spouse.

How does marriage affect the will?: Revokes the will as to the spouse if she or he is not otherwise provided for. Spouse will still be entitled to her or his statutory share under the state intestate laws.

Who must be mentioned in the will?: Children, born or adopted; surviving spouse.

Spouse's right to property regardless of will: The surviving spouse is entitled to 1/3 of the "augmented" estate of the deceased spouse. In general, the "augmented" estate includes both the property that passes under the will and any other property that passes by other "non-will" transfers, such as under the terms of a living trust or a joint tenancy arrangement.

Laws of intestate succession (distribution if decedent leaves no will):

Spouse and children of spouse surviving: All to spouse.

Spouse and children not of spouse surviving: If one child surviving, 1/2 to spouse and 1/2 to child; if more than 1 child surviving, 1/3 to spouse and 2/3 to children equally.

Spouse, but no children or parent(s) surviving: All to spouse.

Spouse and parent(s), but no children surviving: All to spouse.

Children, but no spouse surviving: All to children equally or to their children per stirpes.

Parent(s), but no spouse or children surviving: All to parents equally, or to the surviving parent.

No spouse, children, or parent(s) surviving: All to brothers and sisters equally or their children per stirpes; or if none, 1/2 to paternal and 1/2 to maternal grandparents or their children per stirpes.

Community Property or Common Law state?: Common Law.

State restrictions on gifts to charities?: Yes. If extensive gifts to charities are contemplated, please refer directly to statute or consult an attorney.

State gift, inheritance, or estate taxes: No gift tax; imposes an inheritance tax of up to 16%; imposes state estate tax equal to federal credit for state death taxes less any amounts paid on state inheritance tax. Maximum total state inheritance and state estate tax is equal to the maximum allowable federal estate tax credit for state death taxes.

Nebraska

State law description: Revised Statutes of Nebraska; Chapter 30, Sections 2201+, 2326+.

Court with probate jurisdiction: County Court.

Minimum age for disposing of property by will: 18.

Required number of witnesses: Two. (Three are recommended).

May witnesses be beneficiaries?: Yes. (Not recommended).

Are there provisions for Self-Proving wills?: Yes. (Use the Affidavit in Chapter 6).

Are living wills recognized?: Yes, under the Revised Statutes of Nebraska. (Use the living will form in Chapter 12).

How does divorce affect the will?: Revokes the will as to the divorced spouse.

How does marriage affect the will?: Spouse will still be entitled to her or his statutory share under the state intestate laws.

Who must be mentioned in the will?: Children, born or adopted; surviving spouse.

Spouse's right to property regardless of will: The surviving spouse is entitled to 1/2 of the "augmented" estate of the deceased spouse. In general, the "augmented" estate includes both the property that passes under the will and any other property that passes by other "non-will" transfers, such as under the terms of a living trust or a joint tenancy arrangement.

Laws of intestate succession (distribution if decedent leaves no will):

Spouse and children of spouse surviving: $50,000 and 1/2 of balance to spouse and 1/2 of balance to children.

Spouse and children not of spouse surviving: 1/2 to spouse and 1/2 to children.

Spouse, but no children or parent(s) surviving: All to spouse.

Spouse and parent(s), but no children surviving: $50,000 and 1/2 of balance to spouse and 1/2 of balance to parents or surviving parent.

Children, but no spouse surviving: All to children equally or to their children per stirpes.

Parent(s), but no spouse or children surviving: All to parents equally, or to the surviving parent.

No spouse, children, or parent(s) surviving: All to brothers and sisters equally, or their children per stirpes; or if none, 1/2 to paternal and 1/2 to maternal grandparents or their children per stirpes.

Community Property or Common Law state?: Common Law.

State restrictions on gifts to charities?: No.

State gift, inheritance, or estate taxes: No gift tax; imposes an inheritance tax of up to 18%; imposes state estate tax equal to federal credit for state death taxes less any amounts paid on state inheritance tax. Maximum total state inheritance and state estate tax is equal to the maximum allowable federal estate tax credit for state death taxes.

Nevada

State law description: Nevada Revised Statutes Annotated; Chapters 133.000-150.999.

Court with probate jurisdiction: District Court.

Minimum age for disposing of property by will: 18.

Required number of witnesses: Two. (Three are recommended).

May witnesses be beneficiaries?: No.

Are there provisions for Self-Proving wills?: Yes. (Use the Affidavit in Chapter 6).

Are living wills recognized?: Yes, under the Nevada Revised Statutes Annotated. (Use the living will form in Chapter 12).

How does divorce affect the will?: Revokes the will as to the divorced spouse, if will was signed prior to entry of divorce decree.

How does marriage affect the will?: Revokes the will as to the spouse if she or he is not otherwise provided for. Spouse may still be entitled to her or his statutory share under the state intestate laws.

Who must be mentioned in the will?: Statute contains detailed provisions regarding this. Please refer directly to statute or consult an attorney if this is a critical factor.

Spouse's right to property regardless of will: Community property right to 1/2 of the deceased spouse's "community" property.

Laws of intestate succession (distribution if decedent leaves no will):

Spouse and children of spouse surviving: All of decedent's community property to spouse. If only 1 child is surviving, 1/2 of decedent's separate property to spouse and 1/2 to child or grandchildren per stirpes; if more than 1 child is surviving, 1/3 of separate property to spouse and 2/3 to the children or grandchildren per stirpes.

Spouse and children not of spouse surviving: Same as above for "Spouse and children of spouse surviving".

Spouse, but no children or parent(s) surviving: All of decedent's community property to spouse. 1/2 of decedent's separate property to spouse and 1/2 to brothers and sisters equally or their children per stirpes; or if none, all to spouse.

Spouse and parent(s), but no children surviving: All of decedent's community property to spouse. 1/2 of decedent's separate property to spouse and 1/2 to parents or surviving parent.

Children, but no spouse surviving: All to children or to their children per stirpes.

Parent(s), but no spouse or children surviving: All to parents equally, or to the surviving parent.

No spouse, children, or parent(s) surviving: All to brothers and sisters equally, or their children per stirpes; or if none, to the next of kin.

Community Property or Common Law state?: Community Property.

State restrictions on gifts to charities?: No.

State gift, inheritance, or estate taxes: No gift tax; no inheritance tax; no state estate tax.

New Hampshire

State law description: New Hampshire Revised Statutes; Chapters 547:1+, 551:1+.

Court with probate jurisdiction: Probate Court.

Minimum age for disposing of property by will: 18, or married (any age).

Required number of witnesses: Two (three recommended).

May witnesses be beneficiaries?: Yes, but any gift to a beneficiary who was a witness will be void unless there were also two other disinterested witnesses.

Are there provisions for Self-Proving wills?: Yes. (If you wish to use a Self-proving Affidavit, please consult an attorney).

Are living wills recognized?: Yes, under the "New Hampshire Terminal Care Document Act". (Use the living will form in Chapter 12).

How does divorce affect the will?: Does not revoke the will.

How does marriage affect the will?: Revokes the will if a child is later born to the marriage.

Who must be mentioned in the will?: Children, born or adopted; grandchildren; surviving spouse.

Spouse's right to property regardless of will: Generally, the surviving spouse is entitled to 1/2 of the deceased spouse's estate if there are no children, and only 1/3 if there are children. However, please refer directly to the statute as the provisions are detailed.

Laws of intestate succession (distribution if decedent leaves no will):

Spouse and children of spouse surviving: $50,000 and 1/2 of balance to spouse and 1/2 of balance to children or grandchildren per stirpes.

Spouse and children not of spouse surviving: 1/2 to spouse and 1/2 to children or grandchildren per stirpes.

Spouse, but no children or parent(s) surviving: All to spouse.

Spouse and parent(s), but no children surviving: $50,000 and 1/2 of balance to spouse and 1/2 of balance to parents or surviving parent.

Children, but no spouse surviving: All to children or to their children per stirpes.

Parent(s), but no spouse or children surviving: All to parents equally, or to the surviving parent.

No spouse, children, or parent(s) surviving: All to brothers and sisters equally, or their children per stirpes; or if none, 1/2 to maternal and 1/2 to paternal grandparents or their children per stirpes.

Community Property or Common Law state?: Common Law.

State restrictions on gifts to charities?: No.

State gift, inheritance, or estate taxes: No gift tax; imposes an inheritance tax of up to 15%; imposes state estate tax equal to federal credit for state death taxes less any amounts paid on state inheritance tax. Maximum total state inheritance and state estate tax is equal to the maximum allowable federal estate tax credit for state death taxes.

New Jersey

State law description: New Jersey Revised Statutes; Title 3B: Chapters 3-1+.

Court with probate jurisdiction: Surrogate's Court.

Minimum age for disposing of property by will: 21.

Required number of witnesses: Two. (Three are recommended).

May witnesses be beneficiaries?: Yes. (Not recommended).

Are there provisions for Self-Proving wills?: Yes. (Use the Affidavit in Chapter 6).

Are living wills recognized?: Yes, under the "New Jersey Advanced Directives for Health Care Act". You may use the living will form in Chapter 12.

How does divorce affect the will?: Revokes the will as to the divorced spouse.

How does marriage affect the will?: Spouse shall still be entitled to her or his statutory share under the state intestate laws.

Who must be mentioned in the will?: Children, born or adopted; grandchildren; surviving spouse.

Spouse's right to property regardless of will: The surviving spouse is entitled to 1/3 of the "augmented" estate of the deceased spouse. In general, the "augmented" estate includes both the property that passes under the will and any other property that passes by other "non-will" transfers, such as under the terms of a living trust or a joint tenancy arrangement.

Laws of intestate succession (distribution if decedent leaves no will):

Spouse and children of spouse surviving: $50,000 and 1/2 of balance to spouse and 1/2 of balance to children or grandchildren per stirpes.

Spouse and children not of spouse surviving: 1/2 to spouse and 1/2 to children or grandchildren per stirpes.

Spouse, but no children or parent(s) surviving: All to spouse.

Spouse and parent(s), but no children surviving: $50,000 and 1/2 of balance to spouse and 1/2 of balance to parents or surviving parent.

Children, but no spouse surviving: All to children or to their children per stirpes.

Parent(s), but no spouse or children surviving: All to parents equally, or to the surviving parent.

No spouse, children, or parent(s) surviving: All to brothers and sisters equally, or their children per stirpes; or if none, 1/2 to maternal and 1/2 to paternal grandparents or their children per stirpes.

Community Property or Common Law state?: Common Law.

State restrictions on gifts to charities?: No.

State gift, inheritance, or estate taxes: No gift tax; imposes an inheritance tax of up to 16%; imposes state estate tax equal to federal credit for state death taxes less any amounts paid on state inheritance tax. Maximum total state inheritance and state estate tax is equal to the maximum allowable federal estate tax credit for state death taxes.

New Mexico

State law description: New Mexico Statutes Annotated; Sections 45-2-101+.

Court with probate jurisdiction: Probate or District Court.

Minimum age for disposing of property by will: 18.

Required number of witnesses: Two. (Three are recommended).

May witnesses be beneficiaries?: Yes. (Not recommended).

Are there provisions for Self-Proving wills?: Yes. (Use the Affidavit in Chapter 6).

Are living wills recognized?: Yes, under the "New Mexico Right to Die Act". (Use the living will form in Chapter 12).

How does divorce affect the will?: Revokes the will as to the divorced spouse.

How does marriage affect the will?: Spouse will still be entitled to her or his statutory share under the state intestate laws.

Who must be mentioned in the will?: Children, born or adopted; surviving spouse.

Spouse's right to property regardless of will: Community property right to 1/2 of the deceased spouse's "community" property.

Laws of intestate succession (distribution if decedent leaves no will):

> Spouse and children of spouse surviving: All of decedent's community property to spouse. 1/4 of decedent's separate property to spouse and 3/4 to children or grandchildren per stirpes.

> Spouse and children not of spouse surviving: All of decedent's community property to spouse. 1/4 of decedent's separate property to spouse and 3/4 to children or grandchildren per stirpes.

> Spouse, but no children or parent(s) surviving: All to spouse.

> Spouse and parent(s), but no children surviving: All to spouse.

> Children, but no spouse surviving: All to children equally or to their children per stirpes.

> Parent(s), but no spouse or children surviving: All to parents equally, or to the surviving parent.

> No spouse, children, or parent(s) surviving: All to brothers and sisters equally, or their children per stirpes; or if none, 1/2 to maternal and 1/2 to paternal grandparents or their children per stirpes.

Community Property or Common Law state?: Community Property.

State restrictions on gifts to charities?: No.

State gift, inheritance, or estate taxes: No gift tax; no inheritance tax; imposes state estate tax equal to federal credit for state death taxes.

New York

State law description: New York Consolidated Laws; Estates, Powers, and Trusts.

Minimum age for disposing of property by will: 18.

Required number of witnesses: Two. (Three are recommended).

May witnesses be beneficiaries?: Yes, but any gift to a beneficiary who was a witness will be void unless there were also two other disinterested witnesses.

Are there provisions for Self-Proving wills?: Yes. (Use the Affidavit in Chapter 6).

Are living wills recognized?: Yes, under New York Statutes. (Use the living will form in Chapter 12).

How does divorce affect the will?: Revokes the will as to the divorced spouse.

How does marriage affect the will?: Does not revoke the will. Surviving spouse has right to take elective share of estate.

Who must be mentioned in the will?: Children, born or adopted; surviving spouse.

Spouse's right to property regardless of will: Generally, the surviving spouse is entitled to $50,000.00 or 1/3 of the deceased spouse's estate. However, please refer directly to the statute as the provisions are detailed.

Laws of intestate succession (distribution if decedent leaves no will):

Spouse and children of spouse surviving: $50,000 and 1/2 of balance to spouse and 1/2 of balance to children or grandchildren per stirpes.

Spouse and children not of spouse surviving: Same as above for "Spouse and children of spouse surviving".

Spouse, but no children or parent(s) surviving: All to spouse.

Spouse and parent(s), but no children surviving: $25,000 and 1/2 of balance to spouse and 1/2 of balance to parents or surviving parent.

Children, but no spouse surviving: All to children equally or to their children per stirpes.

Parent(s), but no spouse or children surviving: All to parents equally, or to the surviving parent.

No spouse, children, or parent(s) surviving: All to brothers and sisters equally, or their children per stirpes; or if none, to grandparents equally or their children per capita; or if none, to the next of kin.

Community Property or Common Law state?: Common Law.

State restrictions on gifts to charities?: No.

State gift, inheritance, or estate taxes: Imposes a gift tax; no inheritance tax; imposes a state estate tax of up to 21% or not less than any federal credit for state death taxes.

North Carolina

State law description: North Carolina General Statutes; Chapters 28A-1+,31-1+, 47-1+.

Court with probate jurisdiction: Superior Court.

Minimum age for disposing of property by will: 18.

Required number of witnesses: Two. (Three are recommended).

May witnesses be beneficiaries?: Yes, but any gift to a beneficiary who was a witness will be void unless there were also two other disinterested witnesses.

Are there provisions for Self-Proving wills?: Yes. (Use the Affidavit in Chapter 6).

Are living wills recognized?: Yes, under the "North Carolina Natural Death Act". (Use the living will form in Chapter 12).

How does divorce affect the will?: Revokes the will as to the divorced spouse.

How does marriage affect the will?: Does not revoke the will.

Who must be mentioned in the will?: Children, born or adopted; surviving spouse.

Spouse's right to property regardless of will: Generally, the surviving spouse is entitled to 1/2 of the deceased spouse's estate if there are no children, and only 1/3 if there are children. please refer directly to the statute for details.

Laws of intestate succession (distribution if decedent leaves no will):

Spouse and children of spouse surviving: If only 1 child surviving, $15,000 (from any personal property, if any) and 1/2 of balance to spouse and 1/2 of balance to children or grandchildren per stirpes. If more than one child, $15,000 (from any personal property, if any) and 1/3 of balance to spouse and 2/3 of balance to children or grandchildren per stirpes.

Spouse and children not of spouse surviving: Same as above for "Spouse and children of spouse surviving".

Spouse, but no children or parent(s) surviving: All to spouse.

Spouse and parent(s), but no children surviving: $25,000 (from any personal property, if any) and 1/2 of balance to spouse and 1/2 of balance to parents or surviving parent.

Children, but no spouse surviving: All to children equally or to their children per stirpes.

Parent(s), but no spouse or children surviving: All to parents equally, or to the surviving parent.

No spouse, children, or parent(s) surviving: All to brothers and sisters equally, or their children per stirpes; or if none, 1/2 to maternal and 1/2 to paternal grandparents or their children per stirpes.

Community Property or Common Law state?: Common Law.

State restrictions on gifts to charities?: No.

State gift, inheritance, or estate taxes: Imposes a gift tax; imposes an inheritance tax of up to 17%; imposes a state estate tax equal to federal credit for state death taxes less any amounts paid on state inheritance tax. Maximum total state inheritance and state estate tax is equal to the maximum allowable federal estate tax credit for state death taxes.

North Dakota

State law description: North Dakota Century Code; Chapters 30.1-01+.

Court with probate jurisdiction: County Court.

Minimum age for disposing of property by will: 18.

Required number of witnesses: Two. (Three are recommended).

May witnesses be beneficiaries?: Yes. (Not recommended).

Are there provisions for Self-Proving wills?: Yes. (Use the Affidavit in Chapter 6).

Are living wills recognized?: Yes, under the "North Dakota Rights of Terminally Ill Act". (Use the living will form in Chapter 12).

How does divorce affect the will?: Revokes the will as to the divorced spouse.

How does marriage affect the will?: Spouse will still be entitled to her or his statutory share under the state intestate laws.

Who must be mentioned in the will?: Children, born or adopted; surviving spouse.

Spouse's right to property regardless of will: The surviving spouse is entitled to 1/3 of the "augmented" estate of the deceased spouse. In general, the "augmented" estate includes both the property that passes under the will and any other property that passes by other "non-will" transfers, such as under the terms of a living trust or a joint tenancy arrangement. (Note: On 8/1/95, these provisions will be amended, however the changes were not available at the time of printing.)

Laws of intestate succession (distribution if decedent leaves no will):

Spouse and children of spouse surviving: $50,000 and 1/2 of balance to spouse and 1/2 of balance to children or grandchildren per stirpes.

Spouse and children not of spouse surviving: 1/2 to spouse and 1/2 to children or grandchildren per stirpes.

Spouse, but no children or parent(s) surviving: All to spouse.

Spouse and parent(s), but no children surviving: $50,000 and 1/2 of balance to spouse and 1/2 of balance to parents or surviving parent.

Children, but no spouse surviving: All to children equally or to their children per stirpes.

Parent(s), but no spouse or children surviving: All to parents equally, or to the surviving parent.

No spouse, children, or parent(s) surviving: All to brothers and sisters equally, or their children per stirpes; or if none, 1/2 to maternal and 1/2 to paternal next of kin.

Community Property or Common Law state?: Common Law.

State restrictions on gifts to charities?: No.

State gift, inheritance, or estate taxes: No gift tax; no inheritance tax; imposes state estate tax equal to federal credit for state death taxes.

Ohio

State law description: Ohio Revised Code Annotated; Sections 2101.01+, 2105.01+, 2107.01+.

Court with probate jurisdiction: Court of Common Pleas.

Minimum age for disposing of property by will: 18.

Required number of witnesses: Two. (Three are recommended).

May witnesses be beneficiaries?: Yes, but any gift to a beneficiary who was a witness will be void (beyond what that beneficiary would get as an intestate share) unless there were also two other disinterested witnesses.

Are there provisions for Self-Proving wills?: Yes. (Use the Affidavit in Chapter 6).

Are living wills recognized?: Not by statute. However, you may still use the living will form in Chapter 12.

How does divorce affect the will?: Revokes the will as to the divorced spouse.

How does marriage affect the will?: Does not revoke the will.

Who must be mentioned in the will?: Children, born or adopted; surviving spouse.

Spouse's right to property regardless of will: Generally, the surviving spouse is entitled to 1/2 of the deceased spouse's estate if there are no children, and only 1/3 if there are children. However, please refer directly to the statute as the provisions are detailed.

Laws of intestate succession (distribution if decedent leaves no will):

Spouse and children of spouse surviving: If only one child surviving, $60,000 and 1/2 of balance to spouse and 1/2 of balance to children or grandchildren per stirpes. If more than one child surviving, $60,000 and 1/3 of balance to spouse and 2/3 of balance to children or grandchildren per stirpes.

Spouse and children not of spouse surviving: If only one child surviving, $20,000 and 1/2 of balance to spouse and 1/2 of balance to children or grandchildren per stirpes. If more than one child surviving, $20,000 and 1/3 of balance to spouse and 2/3 of balance to children or grandchildren per stirpes.

Spouse, but no children or parent(s) surviving: All to spouse.

Spouse and parent(s), but no children surviving: All to spouse.

Children, but no spouse surviving: All to children or to their children per stirpes.

Parent(s), but no spouse or children surviving: All to parents equally, or to the surviving parent.

No spouse, children, or parent(s) surviving: All to brothers and sisters equally, or their children per stirpes; or if none, 1/2 to maternal and 1/2 to paternal grandparents or their children per stirpes; or if none, to the next of kin.

Community Property or Common Law state?: Common Law.

State restrictions on gifts to charities?: Yes. If extensive gifts to charities are contemplated, please refer directly to statute or consult an attorney.

State gift, inheritance, or estate taxes: No gift tax; no inheritance tax; imposes a state estate tax of up to 7% or not less than any federal credit for state death taxes.

Oklahoma

State law description: Oklahoma Statutes Annotated; Title 58, Section 1+, Title 84, Sections 1+.

Court with probate jurisdiction: District Court.

Minimum age for disposing of property by will: 18.

Required number of witnesses: Two. (Three are recommended).

May witnesses be beneficiaries?: Yes. (Not recommended).

Are there provisions for Self-Proving wills?: Yes. (Use the Affidavit in Chapter 6).

Are living wills recognized?: Yes, under the "Oklahoma Natural Death Act". (Use the living will form in Chapter 12).

How does divorce affect the will?: Revokes the will as to the divorced spouse.

How does marriage affect the will?: Revokes the will if a child is later born into the marriage.

Who must be mentioned in the will?: Children, born or adopted; surviving spouse.

Spouse's right to property regardless of will: Generally, the surviving spouse is entitled to 1/2 of the deceased spouse's estate if there are no children, and only 1/3 if there are children. However, please refer to the statute for details.

Laws of intestate succession (distribution if decedent leaves no will):

Spouse and children of spouse surviving: If one child, then 1/2 to spouse and 1/2 to child or grandchildren. If deceased had more than one child, then 1/3 to spouse and 2/3 to children or grandchildren per stirpes.

Spouse and children not of spouse surviving: All of property acquired during the marriage by joint effort to spouse, and balance to children and spouse in equal shares.

Spouse, but no children or parent(s) surviving: 1/2 of other property to spouse and 1/3 to maternal and 1/3 to paternal grandparents or their children per stirpes; or if none, to the next of kin.

Spouse and parent(s), but no children surviving: 1/2 of to spouse and 1/2 to parents or surviving parent per stirpes.

Children, but no spouse surviving: All to children equally or grandchildren per stirpes.

Parent(s), but no spouse or children surviving: All to parents equally, or to the surviving parent.

No spouse, children, or parent(s) surviving: All to brothers and sisters equally, or their children per stirpes; or if none, 1/2 to maternal and 1/2 to paternal grandparents or their children per stirpes; or if none, to the next of kin.

Community Property or Common Law state?: Common Law.

State restrictions on gifts to charities?: No.

State gift, inheritance, or estate taxes: No gift tax; no inheritance tax; imposes a state estate tax of up to 15 % but not less that the federal credit for state death taxes.

Oregon

State law description: Oregon Revised Statutes; Chapter 12, Sections 112.015+, 115.000+, 117.000+.

Court with probate jurisdiction: Circuit or County Court.

Minimum age for disposing of property by will: 18 or married (any age).

Required number of witnesses: Two. (Three are recommended).

May witnesses be beneficiaries?: Yes. (Not recommended).

Are there provisions for Self-Proving wills?: Yes. (Use the Affidavit in Chapter 6).

Are living wills recognized?: Yes, under the "Oregon Directive to Physicians Act". (Use the living will form in Chapter 12).

How does divorce affect the will?: Revokes the will as to the divorced spouse.

How does marriage affect the will?: Revokes the will if the maker of the will is survived by a spouse.

Who must be mentioned in the will?: Statute contains detailed provisions regarding this matter. Please refer directly to statute text or consult an attorney if this is a critical factor.

Spouse's right to property regardless of will: The surviving spouse is entitled to up to 1/4 of the deceased spouse's estate, including any property which was received under the deceased's will.

Laws of intestate succession (distribution if decedent leaves no will):

Spouse and children of spouse surviving: All to spouse.

Spouse and children not of spouse surviving: 1/2 to spouse and 1/2 to children or grandchildren per stirpes.

Spouse, but no children or parent(s) surviving: All to spouse.

Spouse and parent(s), but no children surviving: All to spouse.

Children, but no spouse surviving: All to children equally or to their children per stirpes.

Parent(s), but no spouse or children surviving: All to parents equally, or to the surviving parent.

No spouse, children, or parent(s) surviving: All to brothers and sisters equally, or their children per stirpes; or if none, to the next of kin.

Community Property or Common Law state?: Common Law.

State restrictions on gifts to charities?: No.

State gift, inheritance, or estate taxes: No gift tax; no inheritance tax; imposes state estate tax equal to federal credit for state death taxes.

Pennsylvania

State law description: Pennsylvania Consolidated Statutes; Title 20, Sections 101+.

Court with probate jurisdiction: Court of Common Pleas.

Minimum age for disposing of property by will: 18.

Required number of witnesses: Two.

May witnesses be beneficiaries?: Yes. (Not recommended).

Are there provisions for Self-Proving wills?: Yes. (Use the Affidavit in Chapter 6).

Are living wills recognized?: Yes, under the "Pennsylvania Advanced Directive For Health Care Act". However, you may still use the living will form in Chapter 12.

How does divorce affect the will?: Revokes the will as to the divorced spouse.

How does marriage affect the will?: Surviving spouse receives intestate share if marriage took place after will was signed, unless will gives greater share or will was expressly made in contemplation of marriage. Spouse may still be entitled to her or his statutory share under the state intestate laws.

Who must be mentioned in the will?: Children, born or adopted; surviving spouse.

Spouse's right to property regardless of will: The surviving spouse is entitled to 1/3 of the deceased spouse's estate.

Laws of intestate succession (distribution if decedent leaves no will):

Spouse and children of spouse surviving: $30,000 and 1/2 of balance to spouse and 1/2 of balance to children or grandchildren per stirpes.

Spouse and children not of spouse surviving: 1/2 to spouse and 1/2 to children or grandchildren per stirpes.

Spouse, but no children or parent(s) surviving: All to spouse.

Spouse and parent(s), but no children surviving: $30,000 and 1/2 of balance to spouse and 1/2 of balance to parents or surviving parent.

Children, but no spouse surviving: All to children equally or to their children per stirpes.

Parent(s), but no spouse or children surviving: All to parents equally, or to the surviving parent.

No spouse, children, or parent(s) surviving: All to brothers and sisters equally, or their children per stirpes; or if none, 1/2 to maternal and 1/2 to paternal grandparents; or if none, all to aunts and uncles or their children per stirpes.

Community Property or Common Law state?: Common Law.

State restrictions on gifts to charities?: No.

State gift, inheritance, or estate taxes: No gift tax; imposes an inheritance tax of up to 15%; imposes state estate tax equal to federal credit for state death taxes less any amounts paid on state inheritance tax. Maximum total state inheritance and state estate tax is equal to the maximum allowable federal estate tax credit for state death taxes.

Rhode Island

State law description: Rhode Island General Laws; Title 33, Chapters 33-5-1+.

Court with probate jurisdiction: Probate Court.

Minimum age for disposing of property by will: 18.

Required number of witnesses: Two. (Three are recommended).

May witnesses be beneficiaries?: No.

Are there provisions for Self-Proving wills?: Yes. (Use the Affidavit in Chapter 6).

Are living wills recognized?: Not by statute. However, you may still use the living will form in Chapter 12.

How does divorce affect the will?: Revokes the will as to the former spouse.

How does marriage affect the will?: Revokes the will completely.

Who must be mentioned in the will?: Children, born or adopted; grandchildren (if of deceased child); surviving spouse.

Spouse's right to property regardless of will: The surviving spouse is entitled to 1/3 of the deceased spouse's real estate for the rest of his or her life.

Laws of intestate succession (distribution if decedent leaves no will):

Spouse and children of spouse surviving: Real estate: life estate to spouse and balance to children equally or grandchildren per stirpes; Personal property: 1/2 to spouse and 1/2 to children or grandchildren per stirpes.

Spouse and children not of spouse surviving: Same as above for "Spouse and children of spouse surviving".

Spouse, but no children or parent(s) surviving: Real estate: life estate and $75,000 to spouse (if court approves), balance to brothers and sisters equally; or if none, 1/2 to maternal and 1/2 to paternal grandparents; or if none, to aunts and uncles equally or their children per stirpes; or if none, to the next of kin; or if none, to the spouse. Personal property: $50,000 and 1/2 of balance to spouse and 1/2 of balance same as for real estate.

Spouse and parent(s), but no children surviving: Real estate: life estate and $75,000 to spouse (if court approves), balance to parents or surviving parent; personal property: $50,000 and 1/2 of balance to spouse and 1/2 of balance to parents or surviving parent.

Children, but no spouse surviving: All to children or grandchildren per stirpes.

Parent(s), but no spouse or children surviving: All to parents equally, or to parent.

No spouse, children, or parent(s) surviving: All to brothers and sisters equally, or their children per stirpes; or if none, 1/2 to maternal and 1/2 to paternal grandparents; or if none, to the next of kin.

Community Property or Common Law state?: Common Law.

State restrictions on gifts to charities?: No.

State gift, inheritance, or estate taxes: No gift tax; no inheritance tax; imposes state estate tax equal to federal credit for state death taxes.

South Carolina

State law description: Code of Laws of South Carolina Annotated; Title 62, Sections 62-1-100+.

Court with probate jurisdiction: Probate Court.

Minimum age for disposing of property by will: 18.

Required number of witnesses: Two.

May witnesses be beneficiaries?: Generally, Yes. (Not recommended).

Are there provisions for Self-Proving wills?: Yes. (Use the Affidavit in Chapter 6).

Are living wills recognized?: Yes, under the "South Carolina Death With Dignity Act". (Use the living will form in Chapter 12).

How does divorce affect the will?: Revokes the will as to the divorced spouse.

How does marriage affect the will?: Does not revoke the will.

Who must be mentioned in the will?: Children, born or adopted; surviving spouse.

Spouse's right to property regardless of will: The surviving spouse is entitled to 1/3 of the deceased spouse's real estate for the rest of his or her life.

Laws of intestate succession (distribution if decedent leaves no will):

Spouse and children of spouse surviving: 1/2 to spouse and 1/2 to children or grandchildren.

Spouse and children not of spouse surviving: 1/2 to spouse and 1/2 to children or grandchildren.

Spouse, but no children or parent(s) surviving: All to spouse.

Spouse and parent(s), but no children surviving: 1/2 to spouse and 1/2 to parents, brothers, and sisters or their children per stirpes.

Children, but no spouse surviving: All to children equally or to their children per stirpes.

Parent(s), but no spouse or children surviving: All to parents equally, or to the surviving parent if no brothers and sisters.

No spouse, children, or parent(s) surviving: All to brothers and sisters equally, or their children per stirpes; or if none, to lineal ancestors equally or to survivor; or if none, to aunts and uncles equally or their children per stirpes; or if none, to the next of kin.

Community Property or Common Law state?: Common Law.

State restrictions on gifts to charities?: No.

State gift, inheritance, or estate taxes: Imposes a gift tax; no inheritance tax; imposes a state estate tax of up to 8 % but not less that the federal credit for state death taxes.

South Dakota

State law description: South Dakota Codified Laws Annotated; Title 29, Chapters 29-2-1 to 29-6-25.

Court with probate jurisdiction: Circuit Court.

Minimum age for disposing of property by will: 18.

Required number of witnesses: Two. (Three are recommended).

May witnesses be beneficiaries?: No.

Are there provisions for Self-Proving wills?: Yes. (Use the Affidavit in Chapter 6).

Are living wills recognized?: Not by statute. However, you may still use the living will form in Chapter 12.

How does divorce affect the will?: Does not revoke the will.

How does marriage affect the will?: Revokes the will unless provisions are made for children.

Who must be mentioned in the will?: Statute contains detailed provisions regarding this matter. Please refer directly to statute or consult an attorney if this is important.

Spouse's right to property regardless of will: The surviving spouse is entitled to 1/3 of the entire "augmented" estate of the deceased spouse (essentially, all of the property of the decedent).

Laws of intestate succession (distribution if decedent leaves no will):

Spouse and children of spouse surviving: If one child surviving, 1/2 to spouse and 1/2 to child or grandchildren; if more than one child surviving, 1/3 to spouse and 2/3 to child or grandchildren per stirpes.

Spouse and children not of spouse surviving: Same as above for "Spouse and children of spouse surviving".

Spouse, but no children or parent(s) surviving: $100,000 and 1/2 of balance to spouse, 1/2 of balance to brothers and sisters equally or their children per stirpes; or if none, to the spouse.

Spouse and parent(s), but no children surviving: $100,000 and 1/2 of balance to spouse, 1/2 of balance to parents or the surviving parent.

Children, but no spouse surviving: All to children or to their children per stirpes.

Parent(s), but no spouse or children surviving: All to parents equally, or to the surviving parent.

No spouse, children, or parent(s) surviving: All to brothers and sisters equally, or their children per stirpes; or if none, to the next of kin.

Community Property or Common Law state?: Common Law.

State restrictions on gifts to charities?: No.

State gift, inheritance, or estate taxes: No gift tax; imposes an inheritance tax of up to 30%; imposes state estate tax equal to federal credit for state death taxes less any amounts paid on state inheritance tax. Maximum total state inheritance and state estate tax is equal to the maximum allowable federal estate tax credit for state death taxes.

Tennessee

State law description: Tennessee Code Annotated; Title 32, Sections 32-1-101+.

Court with probate jurisdiction: Probate Court.

Minimum age for disposing of property by will: 18.

Required number of witnesses: Two. (Three are recommended).

May witnesses be beneficiaries?: No.

Are there provisions for Self-Proving wills?: Yes. (Use the Affidavit in Chapter 6).

Are living wills recognized?: Yes, under the "Tennessee Right to Natural Death Act". (Use the living will form in Chapter 12).

How does divorce affect the will?: Revokes the will as to the divorced spouse.

How does marriage affect the will?: Revokes the will if a child is later born to the marriage.

Who must be mentioned in the will?: Children, born or adopted; surviving spouse.

Spouse's right to property regardless of will: The surviving spouse is entitled to 1/3 of the deceased spouse's estate.

Laws of intestate succession (distribution if decedent leaves no will):

Spouse and children of spouse surviving: Family homestead and one year's support allowance and one child's share of estate (at least 1/3) to spouse, balance to children equally or grandchildren per stirpes.

Spouse and children not of spouse surviving: Family homestead and one year's support allowance and one child's share of estate (at least 1/3) to spouse, balance to children equally or grandchildren per stirpes.

Spouse, but no children or parent(s) surviving: All to spouse.

Spouse and parent(s), but no children surviving: All to spouse.

Children, but no spouse surviving: All to children equally or to their children per stirpes.

Parent(s), but no spouse or children surviving: All to parents equally, or to the surviving parent.

No spouse, children, or parent(s) surviving: All to brothers and sisters equally, or their children per stirpes; or if none, 1/2 to maternal and 1/2 to paternal grandparents or surviving grandparent; or if none to the children of grandparents per stirpes..

Community Property or Common Law state?: Common Law.

State restrictions on gifts to charities?: No.

State gift, inheritance, or estate taxes: Imposes a gift tax; imposes an inheritance tax of up to 16%; imposes state estate tax equal to federal credit for state death taxes less any amounts paid on state inheritance tax. Maximum total state inheritance and state estate tax is equal to the maximum allowable federal estate tax credit for state death taxes.

Texas

State law description: Texas Statutes and Code Annotated; Probate Title, Chapters 1+.

Court with probate jurisdiction: County or Probate Court.

Minimum age for disposing of property by will: 18, or married (any age), or member of Armed Forces (any age).

Required number of witnesses: Two. (Three are recommended).

May witnesses be beneficiaries?: Generally, yes. (Not recommended).

Are there provisions for Self-Proving wills?: Yes. (Use the Affidavit in Chapter 6).

Are living wills recognized?: Yes, under the "Texas Natural Death Act". (Use the living will form in Chapter 12).

How does divorce affect the will?: Revokes the will as to the divorced spouse.

How does marriage affect the will?: Does not revoke the will.

Who must be mentioned in the will?: Children, born or adopted.

Spouse's right to property regardless of will: Community property right to 1/2 of the deceased spouse's "community" property.

Laws of intestate succession (distribution if decedent leaves no will):

Spouse and children of spouse surviving: 1/2 of community property, 1/3 life estate in separate real property, and 1/3 separate personal property to spouse; balance to children or grandchildren per stirpes.

Spouse and children not of spouse surviving: Same as above for "Spouse and children of spouse surviving".

Spouse, but no children or parent(s) surviving: All community property, all separate personal property and 1/2 separate real property to spouse; balance to brothers and sisters equally or their children per stirpes; or if none, to grandparents or their descendents; or if none, to spouse.

Spouse and parent(s), but no children surviving: All community property, all separate personal property and 1/2 separate real property to spouse; balance to parents (if both surviving); if only one surviving, 1/4 balance to parent and 1/4 to brothers and sisters equally or their children per stirpes; or if none, entire 1/2 to parent.

Children, but no spouse surviving: All to children or to their children per stirpes.

Parent(s), but no spouse or children surviving: If both parents are surviving, all to parents equally; if only one surviving, 1/2 to parent and 1/2 to brothers and sisters equally or their children per stirpes; or if none, all to parent.

No spouse, children, or parent(s) surviving: All to brothers and sisters equally, or their children per stirpes; or if none, 1/2 to maternal and 1/2 to paternal grandparents or their children per stirpes.

Community Property or Common Law state?: Community Property.

State restrictions on gifts to charities?: No.

State gift, inheritance, or estate taxes: No gift tax; no inheritance tax; imposes state estate tax equal to federal credit for state death taxes.

Utah

State law description: Utah Code Annotated; Sections 75-2-101+.

Court with probate jurisdiction: District Court.

Minimum age for disposing of property by will: 18.

Required number of witnesses: Two. (Three are recommended).

May witnesses be beneficiaries?: Yes. (Not recommended).

Are there provisions for Self-Proving wills?: Yes. (Use the Affidavit in Chapter 6).

Are living wills recognized?: Yes, under the "Utah Personal Choice and Living Will Act". (Use the living will form in Chapter 12).

How does divorce affect the will?: Revokes the will as to the divorced spouse.

How does marriage affect the will?: Does not revoke the will.

Who must be mentioned in the will?: Children, born or adopted; grandchildren (if of deceased child); surviving spouse.

Spouse's right to property regardless of will: The surviving spouse is entitled to 1/3 of the deceased spouse's estate.

Laws of intestate succession (distribution if decedent leaves no will):

Spouse and children of spouse surviving: 1/2 to spouse and 1/2 to children or grandchildren per stirpes.

Spouse and children not of spouse surviving: 1/2 to spouse and 1/2 to children or grandchildren per stirpes.

Spouse, but no children or parent(s) surviving: All to spouse.

Spouse and parent(s), but no children surviving: $100,000 and 1/2 of balance to spouse and 1/2 to parents or surviving parent.

Children, but no spouse surviving: All to children equally or to their children per stirpes.

Parent(s), but no spouse or children surviving: All to parents equally, or to the surviving parent.

No spouse, children, or parent(s) surviving: All to brothers and sisters equally, or their children per stirpes; 1/2 to maternal and 1/2 to paternal grandparents or their descendents per stirpes; or if none, to the next of kin.

Community Property or Common Law state?: Common Law.

State restrictions on gifts to charities?: No.

State gift, inheritance, or estate taxes: No gift tax; no inheritance tax; imposes state estate tax equal to federal credit for state death taxes.

Vermont

State law description: Vermont Statutes Annotated; Sections Title 14, Sections 1+.

Court with probate jurisdiction: Probate Court.

Minimum age for disposing of property by will: 18.

Required number of witnesses: Three.

May witnesses be beneficiaries?: No.

Are there provisions for Self-Proving wills?: No. However, you may still use the Self-Proving Affidavit contained in Chapter 6.

Are living wills recognized?: Yes, under the "Vermont Terminal Care Document Act". (Use the living will form in Chapter 12).

How does divorce affect the will?: Does not revoke the will.

How does marriage affect the will?: Does not revoke the will.

Who must be mentioned in the will?: Children, born or adopted; grandchildren (if of deceased child); surviving spouse.

Spouse's right to property regardless of will: If there are none or more than one child of the surviving spouse and the deceased, the surviving spouse is entitled to 1/3 of the deceased spouse's real estate. If there is only one child of the surviving spouse and the deceased, the surviving spouse is entitled to 1/2 of the deceased spouse's real estate. Please refer, however, directly to the statute for instances when this may be barred.

Laws of intestate succession (distribution if decedent leaves no will):

Spouse and children of spouse surviving: If one child surviving: 1/2 of deceased's estate; balance to child or grandchildren per stirpes. If more than one child surviving: 1/3 to spouse and 2/3 to child or grandchildren per stirpes.

Spouse and children not of spouse surviving: If one child surviving: 1/3 of deceased's estate; balance to child or grandchildren per stirpes.

Spouse, but no children or parent(s) surviving: If spouse waives the statutory share and any will provisions, then $25,000 and 1/2 of balance to spouse and 1/2 of balance as if surviving spouse had not survived.

Spouse and parent(s), but no children surviving: $25,000 and 1/2 of balance to spouse and 1/2 of balance as if surviving spouse had not survived.

Children, but no spouse surviving: All to children equally or to their children per stirpes.

Parent(s), but no spouse or children surviving: All to parents equally, or to the surviving parent.

No spouse, children, or parent(s) surviving: All to brothers and sisters equally, or their children per stirpes; or if none, to the next of kin.

Community Property or Common Law state?: Common Law.

State restrictions on gifts to charities?: No.

State gift, inheritance, or estate taxes: No gift tax; no inheritance tax; imposes state estate tax equal to federal credit for state death taxes.

Virginia

State law description: Virginia Code Annotated; Title 64, Sections 64.1-1 to 64.1-180.
Court with probate jurisdiction: Circuit Court.
Minimum age for disposing of property by will: 18.
Required number of witnesses: Two. (Three are recommended).
May witnesses be beneficiaries?: No.
Are there provisions for Self-Proving wills?: Yes. (Use the Affidavit in Chapter 6).
Are living wills recognized?: Yes, under the "Natural Death Act of Virginia". (Use the living will form in Chapter 12).
How does divorce affect the will?: Revokes the will as to the divorced spouse.
How does marriage affect the will?: Does not revoke the will.
Who must be mentioned in the will?: Children, born or adopted; grandchildren (if of deceased child); surviving spouse.
Spouse's right to property regardless of will: The surviving spouse is entitled to 1/3 of the deceased spouse's real estate for the rest of his or her life.
Laws of intestate succession (distribution if decedent leaves no will):
  Spouse and children of spouse surviving: All to spouse.
  Spouse and children not of spouse surviving: 1/3 to spouse and 2/3 to children or grandchildren per stirpes.
  Spouse, but no children or parent(s) surviving: All to spouse.
  Spouse and parent(s), but no children surviving: All to spouse.
  Children, but no spouse surviving: All to children equally or to their children per stirpes.
  Parent(s), but no spouse or children surviving: All to parents equally, or to the surviving parent.
  No spouse, children, or parent(s) surviving: All to brothers and sisters equally, or their children per stirpes; or if none, 1/2 to maternal grandparents or maternal next of kin (or if none, to paternal side) and 1/2 to paternal grandparents, or their children, or paternal next of kin (or if none to maternal side).
Community Property or Common Law state?: Common Law.
State restrictions on gifts to charities?: No.
State gift, inheritance, or estate taxes: No gift tax; no inheritance tax; imposes state estate tax equal to federal credit for state death taxes.

Washington

State law description: Washington Revised Code Annotated; Title 11, Chapters 11.02.001+, 11.12.010+ .

Court with probate jurisdiction: Superior Court.

Minimum age for disposing of property by will: 18.

Required number of witnesses: Two. (Three are recommended).

May witnesses be beneficiaries?: No.

Are there provisions for Self-Proving wills?: Yes. (Use the Affidavit in Chapter 6).

Are living wills recognized?: Yes, under the "Washington Natural Death Act". (Use the living will form in Chapter 12).

How does divorce affect the will?: Revokes the will as to the divorced spouse.

How does marriage affect the will?: Revokes the will as to the surviving spouse.

Who must be mentioned in the will?: Statute contains detailed provisions regarding this matter. Please refer directly to statute text or consult an attorney if this is a critical factor.

Spouse's right to property regardless of will: Community property right to 1/2 of the deceased spouse's "community" property.

Laws of intestate succession (distribution if decedent leaves no will):

Spouse and children of spouse surviving: All of decedent's community property and 1/2 of decedent's separate property to spouse; 1/2 of decedent's separate property to children or grandchildren per stirpes.

Spouse and children not of spouse surviving: All of decedent's community property and 1/2 of decedent's separate property to spouse; 1/2 of decedent's separate property to children or grandchildren per stirpes.

Spouse, but no children or parent(s) surviving: All to spouse.

Spouse and parent(s), but no children surviving: All decedent's community property and 3/4 decedent's separate property to spouse; 1/4 decedent's separate property to parents or surviving parent or their children.

Children, but no spouse surviving: All to children equally or to their children per stirpes.

Parent(s), but no spouse or children surviving: All to parents equally, or to the surviving parent.

No spouse, children, or parent(s) surviving: All to brothers and sisters equally, or their children per stirpes; or if none, to grandparents or their children.

Community Property or Common Law state?: Community Property.

State restrictions on gifts to charities?: No.

State gift, inheritance, or estate taxes: No gift tax; no inheritance tax; imposes state estate tax equal to federal credit for state death taxes.

West Virginia

State law description: West Virginia Code Annotated; Sections 41, 42, 44-1-1.

Court with probate jurisdiction: County Court.

Minimum age for disposing of property by will: 18.

Required number of witnesses: Two. (Three are recommended).

May witnesses be beneficiaries?: No.

Are there provisions for Self-Proving wills?: Yes. (Use the Affidavit in Chapter 6).

Are living wills recognized?: Yes, under the "West Virginia Natural Death Act". (Use the living will form in Chapter 12).

How does divorce affect the will?: Revokes the will completely.

How does marriage affect the will?: Revokes the will completely.

Who must be mentioned in the will?: Children, born or adopted; grandchildren ; surviving spouse.

Spouse's right to property regardless of will: The surviving spouse is entitled to 1/3 of the deceased spouse's real estate for the rest of his or her life.

Laws of intestate succession (distribution if decedent leaves no will):

Spouse and children of spouse surviving: All to spouse.

Spouse and children not of spouse surviving: 3/5 to spouse if all of deceased's children are also children of surviving spouse and surviving spouse also has children who are not deceased's children; balance to deceased's children or grandchildren per stirpes.

Spouse, but no children or parent(s) surviving: All to spouse.

Spouse and parent(s), but no children surviving: All to spouse.

Children, but no spouse surviving: All to children equally or to their children per stirpes.

Parent(s), but no spouse or children surviving: All to parents equally, or to the surviving parent.

No spouse, children, or parent(s) surviving: All to brothers and sisters equally, or their children per stirpes; or if none, 1/2 to maternal grandparents or their children or maternal uncles and aunts or their children, or maternal next of kin (or if none, to paternal side) and 1/2 to paternal grandparents, or their children, or paternal uncles and aunts or their children, or paternal next of kin (or if none to maternal side).

Community Property or Common Law state?: Common Law.

State restrictions on gifts to charities?: No.

State gift, inheritance, or estate taxes: No gift tax; no inheritance tax; imposes state estate tax equal to federal credit for state death taxes.

Wisconsin

State law description: Wisconsin Statutes Annotated; Sections 851.001+, 852.01+, and 853.01+

Court with probate jurisdiction: Circuit Court.

Minimum age for disposing of property by will: 18.

Required number of witnesses: Two. (Three are recommended).

May witnesses be beneficiaries?: No.

Are there provisions for Self-Proving wills?: No. However, you may still use the Self-Proving Affidavit contained in Chapter 6.

Are living wills recognized?: Yes, under the "Wisconsin Natural Death Act". (Use the living will form in Chapter 12).

How does divorce affect the will?: Revokes the will as to the divorced spouse.

How does marriage affect the will?: Revokes the will as to the spouse if she or he is not otherwise provided for. Spouse may still be entitled to her or his statutory share under the state intestate laws.

Who must be mentioned in the will?: Children, born or adopted; grandchildren (if of deceased child); surviving spouse.

Spouse's right to property regardless of will: Modified community property right to 1/2 of the deceased spouse's "community" property.

Laws of intestate succession (distribution if decedent leaves no will):
Spouse and children of spouse surviving: All to spouse.
Spouse and children not of spouse surviving: 1/2 to spouse and 1/2 to children or grandchildren per stirpes.
Spouse, but no children or parent(s) surviving: All to spouse.
Spouse and parent(s), but no children surviving: All to spouse.
Children, but no spouse surviving: All to children or to their children per stirpes.
Parent(s), but no spouse or children surviving: All to parents equally, or to the surviving parent.
No spouse, children, or parent(s) surviving: All to brothers and sisters equally, or their children per stirpes; or if none, to grandparents or surviving grandparent; or if none, to the next of kin.

Community Property or Common Law state?: Common Law. (However, please note that Wisconsin has a marital property act which treats property held in a marriage in essentially the same as it is treated in "Community Property" states. The Wisconsin law, however, uses a unique terminology to describe this treatment of property.

State restrictions on gifts to charities?: No.

State gift, inheritance, or estate taxes: Imposes a gift tax; imposes an inheritance tax of up to 20%; imposes state estate tax equal to federal credit for state death taxes less any amounts paid on state inheritance tax. Maximum total state inheritance and state estate tax is equal to the maximum allowable federal estate tax credit for state death taxes.

Wyoming

State law description: Wyoming Statutes; Title 2, Chapters 2-1-101+.

Court with probate jurisdiction: District Court.

Minimum age for disposing of property by will: 18.

Required number of witnesses: Two. (Three are recommended).

May witnesses be beneficiaries?: No.

Are there provisions for Self-Proving wills?: Yes. (Use the Affidavit in Chapter 6).

Are living wills recognized?: Yes, under the "Wyoming Living Will Act". (Use the living will form in Chapter 12).

How does divorce affect the will?: Revokes the will as to the divorced spouse.

How does marriage affect the will?: Does not revoke the will.

Who must be mentioned in the will?: Statute contains detailed provisions regarding this matter. Please refer directly to statute text or consult an attorney if this is a critical factor.

Spouse's right to property regardless of will: Generally, the surviving spouse is entitled to 1/2 of the deceased spouse's estate if there are no children or if surviving spouse is parent of deceased's children; and only 1/4 if the surviving spouse is not the parent of any surviving children of the deceased. However, please refer directly to the statute as the provisions are detailed.

Laws of intestate succession (distribution if decedent leaves no will):

Spouse and children of spouse surviving: 1/2 to spouse and 1/2 to children or grandchildren per stirpes.

Spouse and children not of spouse surviving: 1/2 to spouse and 1/2 to children or grandchildren per stirpes.

Spouse, but no children or parent(s) surviving: All to spouse.

Spouse and parent(s), but no children surviving: All to spouse.

Children, but no spouse surviving: All to children equally or to their children per stirpes.

Parent(s), but no spouse or children surviving: All to parents, brothers, and sisters equally, or to children of brothers and sisters per stirpes.

No spouse, children, or parent(s) surviving: All to grandparents, uncles, or aunts or their children per stirpes.

Community Property or Common Law state?: Common Law.

State restrictions on gifts to charities?: No.

State gift, inheritance, or estate taxes: No gift tax; no inheritance tax; imposes state estate tax equal to federal credit for state death taxes.

Glossary of Legal Terms

Abatement: A reduction or complete extinguishment of a gift in a will where the estate does not have sufficient assets to make full payment.

Acknowledgement: Formal declaration before a Notary Public.

Ademption: The withdrawal of a gift in a will by an act of the *Testator's* which shows an intent to revoke it. For example; by giving the willed property away as a gift during his or her life.

Administrator/Administratrix: One who is appointed to administer the estate of a deceased person who has died without a will or who has died with a will but has not named an Executor. The distinction between the two titles (male and female) has largely been removed and Administrator is proper usage for either male or female.

Advancement: A lifetime gift made to a child by a parent, with the intent that the gift be all or a portion of what the child will be entitled to on the parent's death.

Ancestor: One from whom a person is descended.

Attestation: To sign one's name as a witness to a will.

Beneficiary: One who is named in a will to receive property; one who receives a benefit or gift, as under the terms of a *trust*.

Bequest: Traditionally, a gift of personal property in a will. Synonymous with legacy. Now, "gift" is the appropriate usage for either a gift of real estate or personal property.

Codicil: A formally signed supplement to a will.

Common Law: System of law which originated in England based on general legal principles rather than legislative acts.

Community Property: The property acquired by either spouse during marriage, other than by gift or inheritance. Each spouse owns a 1/2 interest in the community property. See Appendix for those states in which this system of marital property applies.

Conservator: Temporary court appointed custodian of property.

Curtesy: In ancient common law, a husband's right to all of his wife's real estate for life upon her death. Now generally abolished in most jurisdictions and replaced with a right to a certain *statutory share* of a spouse's property.

Decedent: One who has died.

Descendant: One who is descended from another.

Descent: Inheritance by operation of law rather than by will.

Devise: Traditionally, a gift of real estate under a will. Now, "gift" is the appropriate usage for either a gift of real estate or personal property.

Domicile: A person's principal and permanent home.

Dower: In ancient common law, a wife's right to one-third of her husband's real estate for her life upon his death. Now generally abolished in most jurisdictions and replaced with a right to a certain *statutory share* of a spouse's property.

Escheat: The reversion of property to the state, if there is no family member found to inherit it.

Estate: All property owned by a person.

Execution: The formal signing of a will.

Executor/Executrix: The person appointed in a will to carry out the *testator's* wishes and to administer the property.

Fiduciary: A person with a duty of care to another. For example, a *trustee* has a duty of care to any *beneficiary* of a *trust*, and, thus, is a fiduciary.

Gift: A voluntary transfer of property to another without any compensation.

Guardian: A person with the legal power and duty to care for another person and/or a person's property.

Heirs: Those persons who inherit from a person by operation of law if there is no will present.

Holographic: A will that is entirely handwritten by the *testator* and unwitnessed. No longer valid in most states.

Intestate: To die without leaving a valid will.

Legacy: A gift of personal property in a will. Now, "gift" is the appropriate usage for either a gift of real estate or personal property. Synonymous with bequest.

Letters of Administration: The court order which officially appoints a person to administer the estate of another.

Letters Testamentary: The court order which officially appoints an *executor* named in a will as the person to administer the estate of the *testator*.

Nuncupative: An oral will, usually during a person's last illness and later reduced to writing by another. No longer valid in most states.

Per Capita: Equally; share and share alike. For example: if a gift is made to ones' descendants, per capita, and one has two children and two grandchildren and one of the children dies, then the gift is divided equally among the surviving child and the two grand-children. This amounts to one-third to the child and one-third to each grand-child.

Per Stirpes: To share by representation. For example: if a gift is made to two children, per stirpes, and one should die but leave two grand-children, the deceased child's share is given to the two grand-children in equal shares. This amounts then to one-half to the surviving child and one-fourth to each of the grand-children.

Personal Property: Movable property, as opposed to *real estate*.

Personal Representative: A person who is appointed to administer a deceased's estate. Modern usage which replaces *Executor* and/or *Administrator*.

Posthumous Child: A child born after the father's death.

Pretermitted Child: A child who is left nothing in a parent's will and where there is no intent shown to disinherit.

Probate: The court proceeding to determine the validity of a will and, in general, the administration of the property which passes under the will.

Real Estate/Real Property: Land and that which is attached permanently to it, as opposed to *personal property*.

Residuary: The remainder of an estate after all debts, taxes, and gifts have been distributed.

Revocation: The annulment of a will, which renders it invalid. Accomplished either by complete destruction of the original will or by executing a later will which revokes the earlier one.

Spouse's Share: (See "*Statutory Share*").

Statutory Share: In "common law" states, that portion of a person's property that a spouse is entitled to by law, regardless of any provisions in a will. In "community property" states, a surviving spouse receives 1/2 of all of the community property, regardless of any provisions in a will.

Testamentary: The expression of intent to dispose of property by will.

Testator/Testratrix: A male or female who makes a will.

Trust: In general, property held by one party, the *trustee*, for the benefit of another party, the *beneficiary*.

Trustee: A person appointed to administer a *trust*.

Will: A formally signed and witnessed document by which a person makes a disposition of his or her property to take effect upon death.

Index